Editor

Lorin Klistoff, M.A.

Editor in Chief

Karen J. Goldfluss, M.S. Ed.

Cover Artist

Brenda DiAntonis

Illustrator

Teacher Created Resources Staff

Art Coordinator

Renée Christine Yates

Imaging

Leonard P. Swierski

Publisher

Mary D. Smith, M.S. Ed.

TCR 2433

MW00581332

TARG GRAMMAR

Lessons, practice & MORE!

Includes Standards & Benchmarks

Interactive games & literacy center activities

Ideas for getting students actively involved

Word banks & other handy references

Teacher Created Resources

Author

Teacher Created Resources

Teacher Created Resources, Inc.

6421 Industry Way

Westminster, CA 92683

www.teachercreated.com

ISBN: 978-1-4206-2433-5

© 2009 Teacher Created Resources, Inc.

Made in U.S.A.

Teacher Created Resources

Section 1 CONTENTS

NOUNS

ADJECTIVES

PRONOUNS

Section 1 CONTENTS

VERBS

ADVERBS

SENTENCES

Section 2 CONTENTS

GAMES & ACTIVITIES. 102

Like art and music, language can rise to the highest form of expression. Like art, it has composition, balance, and color. Like music it has rhythm, harmony, and fluidness. And like all art, it can touch the heart and inspire the soul. We speak and our words fade away on a breath. Yet, what impressions we can leave behind!

In a busy modern world, language, in all its technical and creative brilliance, is often outshone by the very stimulating audio-visual world of multimedia. Many of our children are stepping into a world of virtual reality, which only requires their passive acquiescence. As teachers in this modern world, we have to equip our young people with the skills they need to communicate easily and successfully. It is not enough to get by with an oral vernacular and text message shorthand. Employers require workers who can speak eloquently and confidently. They need workers who can write in succinct and precise ways using correct grammar and spelling. Without the facility of using language to express themselves orally and in the written form, people can become excluded and powerless in many areas of business and society.

For too long, the teaching of grammar has been discounted as being outdated and irrelevant. Yet, grammar is at the heart and soul of language. As teachers, we need to help our young people develop the skills they need to express themselves creatively and meaningfully; to be able to critically evaluate the myriad texts that surround them every day. This book is intended for use by teachers to help their students build a strong and solid foundation for language use. It draws on a traditional model relevant to a modern world. We cannot be critical of what we see, hear, and read if we don't know how the creators of text manipulate words and language through their grammatical choices. As teachers, we need to instruct our students in these underlying structures and patterns and ways of making meaning. Part of using text "in context" is to understand how the text itself is created. Grammar does and will continue to play a central role in the composition of our language, both oral and written.

Language has not been "created" for our use. We use it to create our reality, our lives, and our relationships. Without it, we are powerless.

This book presents detailed knowledge of correct English grammar and its application in spoken and written language, relevant to this level of schooling. Both teacher and students can examine and explore language, leading to deeper understandings and improved technique.

Section 1 of this book is divided into the following subsections:

1. Nouns	4. Verbs
2. Adjectives	5. Adverbs
3. Pronouns	6. Sentences

Each subsection contains the following:

A Note to the Teacher   Knowledge of the topic is stripped to its bare bones. This information serves as the basis for the explicit teaching to follow. For some, this will be a refresher course. For others, it may be a first introduction to grammar in all its depth and beauty.

Introducing Ideas   Included in the notes are suggestions for ways of introducing specific grammar concept to students. The ideas begun here are developed in the student pages that follow.

Exploring Ideas   This page offers ideas for getting students actively involved in an exploration of the area of study to build understanding.

Student Pages   The student pages have been designed for students to examine and explore the technical aspects of grammar and its practical application. Scaffolds are in place to support learning with each grammar concept written at the top of each student page. Teachers need to explicitly teach these concepts before presenting the student page to students.

Assessment   Assessment items have marks allocated. The marking system allows the teacher to evaluate, analyze, and pinpoint areas of individual and class need. Reproducible marking grids for each section have been provided on the following pages to assist with monitoring individual students and/or whole-class progress.

Section 2 of this book includes the following:

Games   Ready-to-use games and materials are clearly listed. Directions and suggestions follow for use with small groups of students. Games are an enjoyable way of reinforcing the language students need to successfully use and understand grammar. Group games can help to reinforce students' understanding of grammar and, in many cases, the spelling closely associated with its use.

Task Cards   The task cards have been designed especially for practicing grammatical concepts and knowledge. Like any other endeavor, we need exposure, focused attention, trial and error, application, and technical know-how. Above all, we need to practice what we think we know. Task cards are for individual use. They may be used by all students within a literacy center or by any individual student who requires further practice.

Word Banks   A range of practical reference materials designed to save teacher's time.

Answer Key   There is an answer key for the student pages, the games, and the task cards at the end of the book.

Nouns
pages 32 – 33

Maximum points	5	5	5	5	5	5	5	5	40
	Check 1	Check 2	Check 3	Check 4	Check 5	Check 6	Check 7	Check 8	TOTAL
Student Names	identify nouns	apply spelling rules to form plurals	use apostrophes to show possession	use articles correctly	build compound nouns	identify proper nouns	identify gender nouns	understand concept of noun phrases	

Adjectives
pages 44 – 45

Maximum points	10	10	5	5	6	4	40
	Check 1	Check 2	Check 3	Check 4	Check 5	Check 6	TOTAL
Student Names	identify adjectives	use verbal adjectives to describe nouns	apply knowledge of adjectives of degree	apply knowledge of adjectives to sentence writing	use descriptive adjectives	apply knowledge of adjective/noun relationship	

Pronouns
page 55

	Maximum points	10	10	10	10	40
Student Names		Check 1	Check 2	Check 3	Check 4	TOTAL
		recognize pronouns	apply knowledge of pronouns	understand pronouns/ noun relationship	apply knowledge of pronouns to sentence writing	

Verbs
pages 74 – 75

Maximum points	5	5	5	5	5	5	5	5	40
	Check 1	Check 2	Check 3	Check 4	Check 5	Check 6	Check 7	Check 8	TOTAL
Student Names	identify verbs/verb groups	form contractions	understand subject/ verb agreement ("being" verbs)	form regular/irregular past tense verbs	understand the use of "helping" verbs	understand subject/ verb agreement	select appropriate "saying" verbs	discriminate the use of "did" and "done"	

10

Adverbs
pages 84 – 85

Maximum points	6	5	10	4	5	5	5	40
	Check 1	Check 2	Check 3	Check 4	Check 5	Check 6	Check 7	TOTAL
Student Names	understand the function of adverbs	identify adverbs	use "ly" to form adverbs	use interrogative adverbs	understand adverb/ verb relationship	discriminate between adjective and adverb	choose adverbs appropriate to context	

ASSESSMENT RECORDS

Sentences
pages 99 – 101

Student Names	Maximum points 5	5	3	2	3	2	3	2	2	4	3	6	40
	Check 1	Check 2	Check 3	Check 4	Check 5	Check 6	Check 7	Check 8	Check 9	Check 10	Check 11	Check 12	TOTAL
	identify sentence as a unit	identify subject of sentence	recognize the pattern of a question	apply knowledge of the pattern of a question	recognize the pattern of a command	apply knowledge of the pattern of a command	use conjunctions to form compound sentences	form compound sentences	punctuate a text	apply knowledge of sentence patterns	understand sentence as exclamation	capitalize and punctuate a text	

Summary

Maximum points	40	40	40	40	40	40	240
Student Names	NOUNS	ADJECTIVES	PRONOUNS	VERBS	ADVERBS	SENTENCES	TOTAL

GAMES & ACTIVITIES MATRIX

Focus	Wordworks pages 103–109	Grammar Flaps pages 110–115	GRAND SLAM pages 116–128	Tactics! pages 129–133	Grammar by Numbers pages 134–143	Kriss Kross pages 144–149	TASK CARDS pages 150–161
Adjectives	✓	✓	✓	✓	✓	✓	✓
Adjectives—degree	✓						✓
Adverbs	✓	✓	✓	✓	✓	✓	✓
Antonyms	✓	✓			✓	✓	✓
Articles							✓
Compound sentences							✓
Compound nouns		✓		✓	✓		✓
Conjunctions	✓			✓			✓
Contractions	✓	✓	✓	✓	✓		✓
Dialogue							✓
Gender	✓	✓					✓
Noun phrases	✓						
Nouns	✓	✓	✓	✓	✓	✓	✓
Participles	✓						✓
Phrases	✓						
Plurals	✓	✓					✓
Possessive nouns							✓
Pronouns	✓	✓	✓	✓	✓	✓	✓
Proper nouns							✓
Punctuation							✓
Questions	✓	✓			✓		✓
Sentences					✓		✓
Statements	✓						
Subject/predicate	✓						✓
Subjects	✓	✓					✓
Tense	✓	✓		✓		✓	✓
Verbal adjectives	✓						
Verbs	✓		✓	✓	✓	✓	✓
Verbs—helping	✓	✓					✓
Verbs—doing	✓						
Verbs—saying	✓						

STANDARDS

The lessons and activities in this book meet the following standards and benchmarks, which are used with permission from McREL. (Copyright 2009 McREL. Mid-continent Research for Education and Learning, 4601 DTC Boulevard, Suite 500 Denver, CO 80237 Telephone: 303-337-0990 Website: www.mcrel.org/standards-benchmarks)

Standard 1: Uses the general skills and strategies of the writing process

- Editing and Publishing: Uses strategies to edit and publish written work (e.g., edits for grammar, punctuation, capitalization, and spelling at a developmentally appropriate level; uses reference materials; considers page format [paragraphs, margins, indentations, titles]; selects presentation format according to purpose; incorporates photos, illustrations, charts, and graphs; uses available technology to compose and publish work)

Standard 2: Uses the stylistic and rhetorical aspects of writing

- Uses descriptive language that clarifies and enhances ideas (e.g., common figures of speech, sensory details)

- Uses paragraph form in writing (e.g., indents the first word of a paragraph, uses topic sentences, recognizes a paragraph as a group of sentences about one main idea, uses an introductory and concluding paragraph, writes several related paragraphs)

- Uses a variety of sentence structures in writing (e.g., expands basic sentence patterns, uses exclamatory and imperative sentences)

Standard 3: Uses grammatical and mechanical conventions in written compositions

- Uses pronouns in written compositions (e.g., substitutes pronouns for nouns, uses pronoun agreement)

- Uses nouns in written compositions (e.g., uses plural and singular naming words, forms regular and irregular plurals of nouns, uses common and proper nouns, uses nouns as subjects)

- Uses verbs in written compositions (e.g., uses a wide variety of action verbs, past and present verb tenses, simple tenses, forms of regular verbs, verbs that agree with the subject)

- Uses adjectives in written compositions (e.g., indefinite, numerical, predicate adjectives)

- Uses adverbs in written compositions (e.g., to make comparisons)

- Uses coordinating conjunctions in written compositions (e.g., links ideas to connecting words)

- Uses conventions of spelling in written compositions (e.g., spells high frequency, commonly misspelled words from appropriate grade-level list; uses a dictionary and other resources to spell words; uses initial consonant substitution to spell related words; uses vowel combinations for correct spelling; uses contractions, compounds, roots, suffixes, prefixes, and syllable constructions to spell words)

- Uses conventions of capitalization in written compositions (e.g., titles of people; proper nouns [names of towns, cities, counties, and states; days of the week; months of the year; names of streets, names of countries; holidays]; first word of direct quotations; heading salutation, and closing of a letter)

- Uses conventions of punctuation in written compositions (e.g., uses periods after imperative sentences and in initials, abbreviations, and titles before names; uses commas in dates and addresses and after greeting and closings in a letter; uses apostrophes in contractions and possessive nouns; uses quotation marks around titles and with direct quotations; uses a colon between hour and minutes)

A sentence is a group of words communicating a complete thought.

e.g., Red dust covered the town.

e.g., It leaked through doors and windows.

e.g., Soon it lay thick on tables and chairs.

We speak and, especially, write in sentences. A sentence is made up of a string of words, with each word having a particular job to do. Some words only have one job to do (e.g., *and, the, a, but*)

Others have different jobs in different sentences (e.g., Red dust covered the town. She will dust the tables and chairs.).

Some words, such as pronouns, also link ideas across sentences. Because they refer backwards and forwards to people and things, they tie ideas together and give text fluency and cohesion. A deep understanding of how words work enables speakers and writers to use language to communicate easily and successfully.

NOUNS

Nouns are the words that name the people, places, animals, and things in sentences.

Carl went to the *shop* to buy
person   place
bones for his *dog.*
things   animal

Different nouns have different jobs to do.

Common nouns name the everyday things around us.

e.g., cup, horse, tree, arm, cheese, book, parrot, basket, clock, pie, pencil, car, rabbit, bridge, computer, soup

Proper nouns give people, places, objects, and events their given or special names.

They are easily recognized because they always begin with a capital letter.

e.g., Jane, Mars, Olympic Games, New York City, Grand Canyon, Sunday, Christmas, April, Swan River, India

Compound nouns are made by joining two words together.

e.g., snowflake, heartbeat, tablecloth, sandcastle, butterscotch, basketball

Possessive nouns show ownership. An apostrophe is always used.

e.g., Jack's horse, children's shoes, the teacher's book, Dad's beard, the cats' whiskers, six hens' eggs

Collective nouns are names given to groups of person or things.

e.g., flock (of birds), herd (of cows), crowd (of people), mob (of kangaroos), swarm (of bees)

Verbal nouns are present participles used as nouns.

e.g., Skiing is a winter sport. Let's go bowling. Skating on thin ice is dangerous. Seeing is believing.

Nouns may be singular or plural.

Singular nouns name one thing.

e.g., box, train, football, flower, match, rose

Plural nouns name more than one thing.

e.g., boxes, trains, footballs, flowers, matches, roses

Most plural nouns are formed by adding "s" or "es" to the singular noun.

Some plural nouns are formed by changing the vowels or adding "en."

e.g., foot—<u>feet</u>; man—<u>men</u>; child—<u>children</u>

Some nouns are both singular and plural.

e.g., sheep, fish, deer

Some nouns are only plural.

e.g., pants, scissors, cutlery

A **noun phrase** is a group of words built around a noun.

e.g., a tiny, black <u>spider</u>; a squat, brown <u>teapot</u>; one chocolate and almond <u>cake</u>; long-awaited <u>news</u>; my straw <u>hat</u>

These noun phrases name the participants in the text.

e.g., <u>The three inexperienced schoolboys</u> became lost in the rain forest. <u>Many local people</u> joined in the search for them. They found <u>the cold, hungry, and frightened boys</u> sixteen hours later.

Articles

The articles *a*, *an*, and *the* are often used to introduce noun groups. *A* and *an* are **indefinite articles** because they do not point to a particular thing. *An* is used before a word beginning with a vowel, or an unsounded "h."

e.g., a boy, a dog, a racing car, an egg, an ant, an old man, an opera, an hour

The is a **definite article** because it points to a known or particular thing.

e.g., the sun, the moon, the boy by the door, the house on the hill, the last page

Ideas for introducing nouns

- Tell the students you are going to talk about words. Ask for some examples to make sure they know what you mean by a "word."

- Tell them that the words we use when we speak and when we write have different jobs to do.

- Tell them that today you are going to talk about a group of words that have a very easy job to do. They are called **nouns**. Write this word on the board.

- Continue by saying (and writing) that their job is to name everything.

- Say "Let's think about what nouns can name. They can name <u>people</u>."

Begin a brainstorming chart (see below).

- Ask the students to help you name some people—people in this room, people in the school, people in the street, at home, etc.

- Write lots of words to ensure that the students understand the concept that nouns name people.

- Continue the brainstorming with animals, places, and things.

People	Animals	Places	Things
children	cat	school	blackboard
teacher	dog	home	chalk
boys	horse	house	duster
girls	giraffe	shop	book
sister	elephant	park	bike
brother	cow	farm	car
shopkeeper	emu	river	truck
cashier	parrot	street	tree

Exploring NOUNS

Junk Mail Jobs

Hand out some junk mail catalogs and ask the students, working in pairs, to list as many nouns as they can within a given time limit. Demonstrate by listing some on the board (e.g., carrots, beans, cake, eggs, sheets, radio, wheelbarrow). At the end of the time, lists can be shared with the whole class or in small groups. Lists could be displayed.

Variation: Use magazine pictures instead of junk mail. This will give a wider variation in lists. At a later date, lists could be returned to owners so the words can be sorted into the four categories. The students do this by placing a letter after the word: P = people, A = animals, PL = places, TH = things.

Word Hunters

Divide the class into four groups and give each group a noun category: people, animals, places, or things. Provide paper slips and marker pens. Tell the students to write nouns (no proper nouns) in their category on single slips of paper. You may do this over a couple of 10-minute sessions and collect all slips of paper. At another session, display a large chart, headed with the four noun categories. Give the students some paper slips. In turn, ask them to tell the class a word and its category. If it is right, it is glued on the chart.

Guess What?

Stand before the class and tell the students to look at you. Tell them you are going to walk around the class. When you snap your fingers at a student, each student is to say a noun, the name of something on you (e.g., skirt, ring, hair, shoes). Tell them they are not to repeat a noun that someone else has said. This activity helps them to listen and focus on naming or labeling.

Variation 1: Ask a student to volunteer to stand before the class.

Variation 2: Ask the students to work in groups of six with one in the center. At your signal (e.g., ring a bell), they change the person in the middle, until everyone has had a turn.

Spot the Nouns

Buy some coloring books for very young children that have simple line drawings (or draw your own). Copy some of these drawings, one per pair, and distribute. Review nouns and ask each pair to write as many nouns as they can find in their picture. Some students may find it easier to work in a group of three.

Note: For this activity, do not insist on correct spelling. This is not a spelling lesson.

Scrap It 1

Prepare a class scrapbook entitled "Nouns." Divide the class into small groups of three or four. Allocate a noun category to each group—people, animals, places, and things. Hand out magazines and junk mail catalogs. Ask the students to cut out pictures of things relating to their category. Within the group, they should glue them onto a sheet of paper, and label the picture with a noun (e.g., a lady, a tiger, an island, pizza). These sheets are added to the class scrapbook.

Nouns 1

Words have many different jobs to do.

| Jack | and | his | friend |

| ran | from | the | house. |

The words with the easiest job to do are the **nouns**.
Their job is to name the things around us:
the *people*, the *animals*, the *places*, and the *things*.

1. **Add three more nouns to each column.**

Nouns

People	Animals	Places	Things
sister	bat	park	pizza
teacher	lizard	beach	book
doctor	tiger	home	flower
_____	_____	_____	_____
_____	_____	_____	_____
_____	_____	_____	_____

Nouns 2

Nouns name people, animals, places, and things.

1. Add a noun to finish each sentence.

  a. Mom cooked some _____.

  b. Go and stand by the _____.

  c. I have a pet _____.

  d. Have you met my _____?

  e. I like to play _____.

2. Underline the nouns. Draw a picture for each noun in each box.

  a. Look, the bus is coming.

  b. I gave flowers to the teacher.

  c. The boy has a bat.

3. Write a noun under each picture.

a _____   an _____   the _____

Nouns 3

Nouns name people, animals, places, and things.

1. Put these nouns in their correct places.

soccer	koala	sandwiches	dentist

a. He saw a _____ up a tree.

b. Come and play _____ with me.

c. The _____ filled a hole in my tooth.

d. I have _____ for my lunch.

2. Search for these nouns.

zebra   saucepan

actor   football

school   peanut

crow   fireman

snake   house

L	T	L	O	O	H	C	S
L	N	E	Z	E	B	R	A
A	Y	K	F	Q	I	O	U
B	V	A	Z	U	V	W	C
T	U	N	A	E	P	U	E
O	E	S	U	O	H	O	P
O	H	Q	R	O	T	C	A
F	I	R	E	M	A	N	N

3. Write a sentence about each noun.

clown	mouse	river

_____

_____

NOUNS

Singular and Plural Nouns 1

Nouns can name one thing.
(Examples: dog, house, book)
Nouns can name more than one thing.
(Examples: dogs, houses, books)

Nouns that name more than one are called **plurals**.

To make a plural noun, add "s" or "es."

EXAMPLES

Singular	Plural	Singular	Plural
cup	cups	brush	brushes
dog	dogs	dress	dresses
sister	sisters	peach	peaches
shop	shops	fox	foxes

1. Write the nouns in plural form

   a. one apple   six   _____

   b. one monkey four _____

   c. one spoon   three _____

   d. one box   nine _____

   e. one dish   five _____

   f. one scratch two _____

2. Add a plural ending to the nouns.

   a. Some of the girl____ in my class wear ribbon____ in their hair.

   b. We packed all our old book____ into cardboard box____.

   c. Dad lost the car key____. Mom found them behind some cushion____.

   d. I bought two pear____, three orange____, four banana____, and two peach____.

   e. Bus____ carry many passenger____ every day.

22

Singular and Plural Nouns 2

Some singular nouns have to change their spelling before adding "es" to make a plural. (Examples: lady—ladies, leaf—leaves)

NOUNS

> **Words that end in a "y"**
> - If the letter before the "y" is a consonant, change the "y" to "i" and add "es."
>   (Examples: baby—<u>babies</u>, tabby—<u>tabbies</u>)
> - If the letter before the "y" is a vowel, just add "s."
>   (Examples: key—<u>keys</u>, boy—<u>boys</u>)

1. **Write the plural of the noun in parentheses.**

   a. There are many _____ (country) in the world.

   b. The _____ (lady) had _____ (key) to their cars.

   c. We saw four _____ (donkey) on the farm.

   d. Mary picked _____ (daisy) and _____ (pansy).

   e. After the storm, the _____ (gully) were filled with water.

> **Words that end in "f" or "fe"**
> - Change the "f" to "v" and add "es."
>   (Examples: loaf—<u>loaves</u>, life—<u>lives</u>)
> - Some don't follow the rule.
>   (Examples: chief—<u>chiefs</u>, roof—<u>roofs</u>)

2. **Change the underlined words to their plural form in the sentences.**

   a. <u>wolf</u>   They could hear the howling of _____.

   b. <u>knife</u>   Put _____ and forks on the table.

   c. <u>leaf</u>   Golden autumn _____ are falling from the trees.

   d. <u>calf</u>   Many _____ were born last spring.

   e. <u>loaf</u>   The baker sold many _____ of fresh brown bread.

NOUNS

Singular and Plural Nouns 3

Some plural nouns are not made by adding "s" or "es."
(Examples: one man—many men, one mouse—six mice)

1. Match the nouns to their plural form.

a. tooth   children

b. goose   women

c. man   geese

d. foot   teeth

e. woman   men

f. child   feet

2. Rewrite the sentences in plural form.

a. The child went with the lady.

_____

b. The autumn leaf fell onto the red roof.

_____

_____

c. My sister ate the peach in the dish.

_____

3. Search out the plurals of these nouns.

brush
rabbit
body
bus
leaf
stitch
cow

l	v	b	r	u	s	h	e	s	g	h	t
e	z	l	w	h	y	f	t	c	o	w	s
a	s	t	i	t	c	h	e	s	n	b	f
v	t	d	r	a	b	b	i	t	s	p	m
e	m	b	n	g	b	o	d	i	e	s	b
s	p	b	u	s	e	s	t	r	e	w	j

Proper Nouns

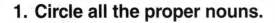

Nouns give people, places, objects, and events their proper names.
(Example: <u>Jack</u> and <u>Jill</u> went to the <u>Olympic Games</u> in <u>Sydney</u>.)

NOUNS

Proper nouns always begin with a capital letter.

1. Circle all the proper nouns.

   a. Anthony lives in Chicago and goes to Cottonwood Elementary School.

   b. My birthday was on the last Saturday in March.

   c. Last Christmas, we went to Hawaii for vacation.

   d. David bought a pair of shoes from T-mart.

   e. Kim flew to Germany to play in the World Cup.

2. Give each proper noun a capital letter.

   a. Many tourists come to disneyland during june.

   b. jack's favorite book character is harry potter.

   c. shymal left his home in India to live in texas.

   d. As you sail into new york, you will see the statue of liberty.

3. Write a sentence using one of these proper nouns.

   Easter   George Washington   Japan   Hollywood

   _____

   _____

NOUNS

Compound Nouns

A **compound noun** is made up of two other nouns. (Examples: cow + boy = cowboy, moon + light = moonlight, egg + shell = eggshell)

1. Join the two words that make a compound noun.

a. hay   brush   _____

b. kick   room   _____

c. tooth   ball   _____

d. bed   stack   haystack

e. foot   boxing   _____

2. Color the two words that make a compound noun. Use different colors.

grand	sun	fall	flakes	stick	hill
shine	side	corn	stand	broom	water

3. Write a sentence for each compound noun.

a. doorbell   _____

_____

b. horseback   _____

_____

c. teapot   _____

_____

Possessive Nouns

Possessive nouns show ownership.
(Examples: <u>Pam's</u> basket, <u>Cory's</u> cat,
the <u>boy's</u> hat, <u>hen's</u> feathers)

NOUNS

You need to use an apostrophe and an "s."   Jana<u>'s</u> house   Carl<u>'s</u> tent
the dog<u>'s</u> bones   my friend<u>'s</u> hair

1. Underline the possessive nouns.

a. Where is Harry's football?

b. I put on Tegan's hat by mistake.

c. That is Dylan's model plane.

d. What is Priya's last name?

e. Mom's new dress is blue.

2. Add *'s* to the underlined nouns to show ownership.

a. Mom found my <u>brother</u>   socks.

b. Which is <u>Maria</u>   house?

c. The <u>sailor</u>   hat blew overboard.

d. She couldn't read the <u>teacher</u>   writing.

e. A <u>parrot</u>   feathers are very colorful.

3. Write a sentence about a fairy's wand or a pirate's sword.

_____

_____

4. Draw these possessive nouns.

your aunt's car	your friend's pet	your teacher's face

NOUNS

Plural Possessive Nouns

For more than one owner, the apostrophe follows the plural noun. (Examples: one boy's book—all the <u>boys'</u> books, my friend's bike—my three <u>friends'</u> bikes)

1. Do the underlined nouns show one owner or more than one owner?

a. The butcher sells <u>dogs'</u> bones. _____

b. <u>Jockeys'</u> shirts are made of silk. _____

c. The <u>girl's</u> pet rabbit is white. _____

d. <u>Birds'</u> feathers lay under the tree. _____

e. I climbed onto the <u>horse's</u> back. _____

2. Add apostrophes correctly to show ownership.

a. We heard the sound of wild horses hooves.

b. Most of the cups handles are broken.

c. The cars tire is flat.

d. All the swimmers times have improved.

e. An eagles wings are very long.

3. Rewrite the possessive nouns in plural form.

a. one lion's tail   two _____ tails

b. an elephant's trunk   ten _____ trunks

c. a crocodile's tooth   many _____ teeth

d. the teacher's car   the _____ cars

e. my cousin's hobby   my _____ hobbies

Gender Nouns

Gender nouns are used to show the difference between male and female. Male is called <u>masculine</u>. Female is called <u>feminine</u>.
(Examples: boy—masculine, girl—feminine; bull—masculine, cow—feminine)

NOUNS

1. Color the matching masculine and feminine nouns. Use a different color for each pair.

bull	man	ram	king	uncle	stallion
aunt	queen	mare	cow	ewe	woman

2. Draw one of these pairs.

lady and gentleman

prince and princess

hen and rooster

Many gender nouns are both male and female.
(Examples: An <u>author</u> can be either male or female.
A <u>writer</u> can be either male or female.)

3. Color the nouns that can be either male or female.

teacher	madam	athlete	doctor	emperor	poet
grandmother	instructor	cowboy	wife	thief	husband

NOUNS

Noun Phrases

A **noun phrase** is a group of words built around a noun.
(Examples: a friendly person; my favorite book; her old, blue slippers; his pet rabbit)

1. Complete these sentences using noun phrases from the boxes below.

a big gray seagull	a new green jacket	a black mountain bike
the strong elephant	a mean, old fox	the sweet plums

a. Tommy arrived on _____.

b. _____ prowled around the henhouse.

c. Jackson and Emily ate _____.

d. _____ came to drink at the water hole.

e. _____ lifted the heavy log.

f. I have _____.

2. Put a box around the noun phrases in these sentences.

a. We watched an interesting television show.

b. The black and white magpie flew back to its tree.

c. He gave me a box of chocolates.

d. I bought a box of cornflakes and a bottle of milk.

3. Write two sentences using the noun phrases listed below.

the lost little kitten   a mysterious package

_____

_____

_____

_____

30

Articles

The words **a**, **an**, and **the** signal that a noun is coming up. (Examples: <u>a</u> red ball, <u>an</u> orange, <u>the</u> wild horses)

"The" points to <u>definite</u> things.

The words "a" and "an" point to only one <u>indefinite</u> thing.

1. The articles "a," "an," and "the" signal nouns. Draw a box around the nouns.

a. The children waited for a ride on the Ferris wheel.

b. We saw a horse in the pasture.

c. A noisy boy chased away the birds.

d. We went to train at the pool for an hour.

e. The girl ate a cookie and an orange.

2. Choose "a" or "an" to complete the sentences.
(*Note:* Using "a" or "an" depends upon the beginning sound of the next word.)

a. I put _____ egg in _____ pot of boiling water.

b. We saw _____ zebra and _____ elephant at _____ zoo.

c. He is _____ odd person.

d. Mom made _____ apple pie and _____ chocolate cake.

e. He is _____ honest boy.

3. Choose "a" or "the" to complete the sentences.

a. I had _____ cup of tea out on _____ deck.

b. _____ children looked for _____ toy in _____ shop.

c. All _____ bikes were painted _____ bright blue.

d. Put _____ lid back on _____ saucepan.

e. I want _____ computer game for my birthday.

Assessment - Nouns

CHECK 1: Circle all the nouns in this text.   ☐ /5

Jamie has twelve wooden soldiers. They all have painted red coats and black pants. He keeps them in an old tin box.

CHECK 2: Write a plural form of these words.   ☐ /5

a. bench   *b.* clock   *c.* lady

_____   _____   _____

d. game   *e.* leaf

_____   _____

CHECK 3: Add apostrophes to show ownership.   ☐ /5

a. The girls hair is brown and curly.

b. The fishermens nets are hanging out to dry.

c. The cats eyes closed, and she fell asleep.

d. All the kids bikes are in the bike rack.

e. We all like to see Katies big smile

CHECK 4: Add "a," "an," or "the" to signal the nouns.   ☐ /5

a. Put _____ clean plates away, please.

b. Mom bought _____ new red dress.

c. _____ winning team received _____ silver cup.

d. He is _____ old friend of mine.

NOUNS

CHECK 5: Write five compound nouns using the words below. (Words can be used more than once.) ☐/5

house	play	light	farm	line
day	sun	life	time	yard

_____

_____

CHECK 6: Write the capital letters for the proper nouns. ☐/5

  a. We traveled to townsville by train.

  b. I gave jordan a box of chocolates.

  c. During easter vacation, we are going to the mountains.

  d. My cousin arrives from france in september.

CHECK 7: Color the matching gender nouns—masculine and feminine. Use a different color for each pair. ☐/5

princess	man	rooster	mother	bull
hen	father	prince	cow	woman

CHECK 8: Complete the sentences with a noun phrase. ☐/5

  a. I opened the box and saw _____.

  b. There was _____ in the pasture.

  c. _____ barked at the tabby cat.

  d. I bought _____ from the supermarket.

  e. Can you see _____?

Student Name: _____

Date: _____   Total Score: _____/40

Adjectives are words that give color, shape, size, sound, and feeling to nouns. Their job is to paint clearer pictures of nouns.

A Note to the Teacher

Speakers and writers create images of people and things through their choice of adjectives.

Adjectives give meaning and life to nouns. They are often chosen specifically to give a positive or a negative view of people, places, events, and objects.

Advertisers know this very well and choose adjectives that will display their products in the most desirable way. They use words like *reliable, charming, immaculate, heavy-duty,* etc. Value can be *outstanding, great,* or *unbeatable.*

The media, too, selects adjectives designed to sway the audience to a particular view. Of a dictator, it may use words like *evil, vicious, ruthless,* and the acts of such a person may be described as *despicable, brutal, inhuman.* Whereas, a princess may be described as *beautiful, stylish, graceful,* performing acts that are *generous, compassionate,* and *admirable.*

Adjectives give life and personality to all the people and things we speak and write about.

Carl, a tall man, went to the local shop to buy big bones for his shaggy, brown dog.

Adjectives are very powerful tools used by writers and speakers.

Adjectives can be placed before the noun they describe.

e.g., I stroked the soft fur of the tiny, white kitten.

Adjectives can be placed after the noun they describe.

e.g., The door was wooden and heavy.
The orange is sweet and juicy.

Different adjectives have different jobs to do.

Descriptive adjectives give color, shape, size, and feeling to nouns.

e.g., sharp pencil
choppy seas
haunting melody
scruffy dog
long, dusty road
quaint, whitewashed cottages

Verbal adjectives are participles used as adjectives. Participles end in *–ing* or *–ed.*

e.g., a walking stick; falling rocks; a deafening roar; scented roses; a puzzled look; a dazed expression

Number adjectives give quantity to the noun.

e.g., ten geese, five marbles, sixth person, first place

Adjectives may show degree.

Adjectives of degree may describe nouns as they are (positive degree)

e.g., I have a long rope,

or compared to another (comparative degree)

e.g., My rope is longer than yours,

or compared to all others (superlative degree)

e.g., Todd has the longest rope of all.

The word endings (suffixes) *–er* and *–est* are usually used to make adjectives of degree.

e.g., old, older, oldest;
big, bigger, biggest;
funny, funnier, funniest

Antonyms show opposite ways of describing nouns.

Because the work of adjectives is to describe nouns, it is possible to use them in ways that will give opposing views of people and things. These adjectives are called **antonyms**.

e.g., a short/tall person
fresh/stale cake
sweet/sour oranges
rough/smooth road
dull/bright day

Ideas for introducing adjectives

- Ask the students to name some objects in the room and make a list on the side of the board.

  e.g., clock, desk, chair, book, door, pencils, boy

- Select one and write a "bare bones" sentence on the board.

  e.g., The boy is by the door.

- Ask the students to give you a word that you could add to describe the boy, to say what he looks like.

  e.g., tall

- Rewrite the sentence:

  The tall boy is by the door.

  Invite them to think of other words. Write them in a list underneath *tall*. Prompt them with thoughts of color, size, weight, etc. (e.g., smart, quiet, clever, naughty) Ask different students to read the new sentences.

- Introduce the word *adjective*, a word used to describe a noun. Writers (and speakers) use them to paint pictures of the people and things they are talking about. Readers (and listeners) will get a much clearer picture of a person, place, or thing if you paint a good picture. Adjectives will help you do this.

- Repeat this process with the word *door*.

  e.g., The tall boy is by the classroom door.

- Ask the students to write any one combination of sentences you have just studied.

- Write the sentence on the board:

  The little dog jumped over the high wall.

  Invite the students to write two or three sentences changing only the words *little* and *high*. Share the results.

- Ask the students to select another word from the list of familiar objects. Ask them to write a "bare bones" sentence, then list some adjectives they could add to paint a better picture of each noun. Share their work.

- Discuss how we tend to describe things by using our senses—seeing, hearing, touching, smelling, tasting—and by the way we feel inside. Ask them to describe an object using their different senses.

  seeing (a man): tall, stooped, old, tired, busy

  hearing (an insect): buzzing, chirping, singing, hissing, growling

  tasting (a fruit): sweet, juicy, sour, crunchy, tangy, bitter

  touching (a stone): rough, smooth, coarse, cold, gritty

  smelling (a room): musty, fresh, smoky, stinking, dusty

  feelings: angry, unhappy, disappointed, sad, glad, excited

- Tell students that using their senses will help them to think of the adjectives that will best describe the people, places, and things they are writing (or speaking) about.

Exploring ADJECTIVES

Sentence Expanders

Divide the class into small groups. Give each group a "bare bones" sentence strip.

e.g., The dog jumped over the wall.

Ask each member of the group to expand the sentence by adding one or two adjectives to describe each noun. Demonstrate this on the board.

e.g., The <u>little</u> dog jumped over the <u>high</u> wall.

Students may orally discuss some ideas before starting, but they should try to write unique sentences. Set a time limit of about eight minutes, before asking the different groups to share their work orally with the whole class.

Adjective Alert

Make enlarged copies of some descriptive texts (e.g., story settings, character descriptions, real estate advertisements). Ask student to work in pairs to discuss and highlight a given number of adjectives (up to 10, depending on the text). On completion, ask the groups to report their findings. Ask class members to check whether the selected words are used as adjectives.

Scrap It 2

Prepare a class scrapbook entitled "Adjectives." Divide the class into small groups of three or four.

Allocate a noun category to each group— people, animals, places, and things. Hand out magazines and junk mail catalogs. Ask the students to cut out pictures of things relating to their categories. Within the group, they should glue them onto a sheet of paper, and label the picture with a noun and a descriptive adjective (e.g., a busy lady, a fierce tiger, a peaceful island, tasty pizza). These sheets are added to the class scrapbook.

Colorful Characters

Give each student one magazine picture. It might be an object (e.g., car, washing machine, boat); or a person (e.g., cook, model, athlete); or a place (e.g., beach, river, store); or an animal (e.g., camel, horse, dog, kitten). Ask each student to glue the picture in the center of a sheet of paper and label it with a noun below the picture. Ask each student to make a web of describing words around the picture. The students can present and display their work at the end of the lesson.

Descriptive Adjectives 1

An **adjective** is a word used to describe a noun. (Examples: an <u>angry</u> person, a <u>happy</u> person, a <u>strong</u> person)

ADJECTIVES

1. Add one or two adjectives to describe each noun.

a _____ clown	a _____ mouse
a _____ elephant	a _____ car

2. Complete the adjectives and place them in the puzzle.

a—across   b_____ bee

b—down   s_____t apple

c—down   s_____ fox

d—across   pr_____ flower

e—down   t_____ tree

f—across   f_____ pig

g—across   l_____ snake

3. We can place an adjective in front of the noun that we want to describe. Write an adjective in each space to describe the nouns.

a. I gave her a bunch of _____ flowers.

b. We looked up at the _____ building.

c. The _____ boy rushed out and slammed the door.

d. I sleep in a _____ bed with a _____ pillow.

e. The _____ camel bent down on its knees.

Descriptive Adjectives 2

Adjectives are used to describe nouns. (Examples: a <u>red</u> ball, a <u>large</u> house, <u>tasty</u> food, a <u>noisy</u> truck, <u>beautiful</u> weather)

1. Circle the three best words on each line that could describe the noun.

a. orange	round	tall	juicy	sweet	brave
b. book	heavy	interesting	hungry	thick	desperate
c. trees	shiny	flowering	leafy	friendly	green
d. kitten	soft	playful	bearded	straw	furry
e. sandwich	plastic	cheese	rocky	fresh	tasty

2. We can place an adjective after the noun that we want to describe. Circle the adjectives that describe the underlined nouns.

a. Our <u>teacher</u> is patient and kind.

b. My <u>puppy</u> is playful.

c. After a long day in the fields, the <u>farmer</u> was tired.

d. The <u>cake</u> was chocolate with white icing.

e. The <u>hens</u> in the hen house were noisy.

3. Write in each space a suitable adjective from the list below.

Josh was in a hurry! He and his **a** _____ friends had made a
b _____ canoe, and it was the day of the **c** _____ race.
He ran down to the **d** _____ shed and dragged out his own canoe.
His **e** _____ dog, Rusty, barked around his feet.

a.	hairy	school	thick
b.	large	rocky	straw
c.	car	boat	tiny
d.	tin	brick	straw
e.	purple	fresh	faithful

Descriptive Adjectives 3

Adjectives work with nouns to give clear pictures of people, places, and things.

ADJECTIVES

1. **Complete the sentences using adjectives.**

   a. The man drove his _____ car along the _____ road.

   b. My _____ brother likes _____ cookies.

   c. The oranges are _____ and _____.

   d. I picked some _____ flowers for my mom.

   e. _____ trees grow in our _____ garden.

2. **Read the story below. When you come to a blank, close your eyes and point to the words at the bottom of the page. This is the word you use in the blank space. Read the story many times and you will have many different, funny stories.**

   Wriggly Wraggly Worm was _____ and _____.
   He lived in the _____ earth under the _____ ferns
   in the _____ garden. One _____ day he wriggled
   out of the _____ dirt and into the _____ flower
   bed. Nothing moved. Wriggly Wraggly Worm did not know that there was a
   _____ bird hiding in the _____ bushes. Before he could
   turn back, the _____ bird swooped down and picked him up in her
   _____ beak.

fat	*hot*	*strong*	*stupid*	*prickly*	*noisy*
green	*angry*	*slimy*	*fine*	*wicked*	*pretty*
clumsy	*ugly*	*lovely*	*sweet*	*dangerous*	*silly*
wild	*brown*	*damp*	*thick*	*huge*	*thorny*

Number Adjectives

Adjectives show number.
(Examples: <u>six</u> buns, <u>two</u> hands, <u>first</u> place, <u>twenty</u> dollars, <u>last</u> chance)

ADJECTIVES

> If we are unsure of the exact numbers, we use: *some   few   many   most*

1. **Complete these sentences using number adjectives.**

   a. I have _____ feet, _____ arms, and _____ legs.

   b. A spider has _____ legs.

   c. Horses have _____ eyes, _____ ears, and _____ legs.

   d. An ant and a hornet both have _____ legs.

   e. A fly has _____ eyes.

   f. There were _____ green ants under the rock.

   g. I only have a _____ chips left.

Adjectives show color, size, and shape. (Examples: <u>red</u> apples, <u>green</u> trees, <u>large</u> animals, <u>tiny</u> ants, <u>round</u> coins, <u>crooked</u> line)

2. **Sort these adjectives into the correct columns.**

   round   brown   small   circular   tiny

   orange   large   square   purple   huge

   triangular   oval   yellow   enormous   scarlet

Color	Size	Shape

Antonyms

Adjectives can describe people and things in opposite ways. (Examples: <u>happy</u> face—<u>sad</u> face, <u>old</u> books—<u>new</u> books, a <u>long</u> road—a <u>short</u> road)

These adjectives are called **antonyms**.

ADJECTIVES

1. Write antonyms (opposites) for these adjectives.

    a. clean _____   *c.* narrow _____   *e.* little _____

    b. high _____   *d.* fresh _____   *f.* short _____

2. Now complete these sentences by using the correct antonyms.

    a. My hands were clean, but now they are _____.

    b. I sat on a _____ stool, and the baby sat in a high chair.

    c. The river is wide, but the creek is _____.

    d. An elephant has _____ ears, but a kitten has little ears.

    e. Do you want a short or a _____ piece of string?

    f. The bread is fresh, but the buns are _____.

3. Search for the antonyms of these adjectives.

    a. slow _____

    b. tall _____

    c. high _____

    d. sad _____

    e. heavy _____

    f. smooth _____

    g. new _____

    h. soft _____

S	L	P	H	A	R	D
D	O	L	D	X	O	L
T	W	G	Y	P	U	Q
S	H	O	R	T	G	Z
A	Y	P	P	A	H	R
F	S	L	I	G	H	T

Verbal Adjectives

Some verbs can be used as adjectives. Many of these **verbal adjectives** end in *–ing* and *–ed*. (Examples: <u>melting</u> snow, <u>dancing</u> partner, <u>grated</u> cheese, <u>parked</u> cars)

ADJECTIVES

1. **Color the matching adjectives and nouns. Use a different color for each pair.**

racing	waiting	interesting	roasted	buttered	baked
peanuts	beans	bikes	books	room	bread

2. **Now use three pairs of words in sentences.**

   a. _____

   b. _____

   c. _____

3. **Make a drawing of two of the noun phrases below.**

walking shoes
a painted face
twinkling stars
an iced cake
a jumping rope
a swimming pool
a striped shirt
a barking dog

Adjectives of Degree

Adjectives show how people and things compare with each other. (Examples: John is <u>tall</u>, but Bill is <u>taller</u>. Jack is the <u>tallest</u> of them all.)
To show degree we usually add *–er* and *–est*.

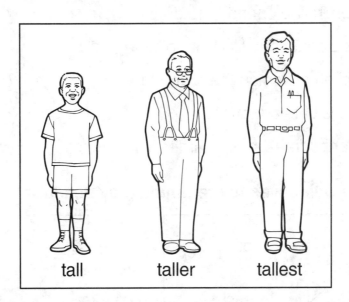

tall   taller   tallest

1. Complete the table of adjectives of degree.

Adjective	–er	–est
loud	louder	loudest
short		
safe		
wet		
low		
large		

2. Color the matching adjectives of degree in the same color.

Adjective	–er	–est
long	older	bravest
old	longer	softest
sharp	softer	wildest
wild	braver	sharpest
soft	sharper	oldest
brave	wilder	longest

3. Add *–er* or *–est* to complete the adjectives correctly.

   a. I have a small dog, but Joanna's dog is small_____ .

   b. Who is the fast_____ person in your class?

   c. Theo and I are young, but I think you are the young_____.

   d. Are you old_____ than your sister?

Assessment--Adjectives

CHECK 1: Find all the adjectives. Circle them. ☐ /10

   a. The lost key was never found.

   b. The first person in line opened the door.

   c. I like scrambled eggs, but Jill likes boiled eggs.

   d. He stacked seven plates on the round table.

   e. Her new dress is blue and white.

   f. We have flowering trees in our garden.

CHECK 2: Join the adjectives to the nouns they describe. ☐ /10

a. dancing	gum	*g.* loaded	fish
b. cooking	stick	*h.* parked	cream
c. building	shoes	*i.* whipped	cheese
d. chewing	pots	*j.* grated	truck
e. walking	sun	*k.* potted	plant
f. setting	blocks	*l.* grilled	cars

CHECK 3: Underline the correct adjective in the parentheses. ☐ /5

   a. A whale is (large larger largest) than an elephant.

   b. Death Valley is one of the (hot hotter hottest) places on Earth.

   c. The sloth is the (slow slower slowest) animal I know.

   d. My jump rope is (long longer longest) than yours.

   e. The fog has become so (thick thicker thickest) I can't see.

Assessment - Adjectives

CHECK 4: Write a sentence about each picture. Include at least two adjectives in each sentence. ☐ /5

a.	b.	c.	d.	e.

a. _____

b. _____

c. _____

d. _____

e. _____

CHECK 5: Fill in the blanks using adjectives. ☐ /6

Taffy was a _____ mouse. He had a _____ tail with a

_____ tip. Taffy loved to tease Mungo, the _____ cat. He would

wait till Mungo was asleep, then pull his _____ whiskers. When Mungo

woke up, no one would be there. Taffy would be hiding under a _____ chair.

CHECK 6: What noun do you think each set of adjectives describes? Write your answers on the line. ☐ /4

a. sweet	b. round	c. sandy	d. tall
juicy	beach	hot	green
red	rubber	wide	shady
crunchy	big	waterless	leafy
_____	_____	_____	_____

Student Name: _____

Date: _____

Total Score: _____/40

PRONOUNS

Pronouns are the words that are used instead of nouns in text. They can be singular or plural, masculine or feminine, and they do the same work as nouns.

Texts, both spoken and written, are made up of sentences whose ideas connect to each other in meaningful ways.

Pronouns are used to replace nouns to avoid the monotony of repetition.

Sarah lost her hat in the park.
Mark said that he would help her look for it.
He said that it was bright red, so they should find it easily.

These pronouns refer back to nouns already mentioned and give the text fluency and cohesion.

Pronouns have three different forms:

First-person pronouns are used when a writer, a speaker, or character is doing the "talking."

e.g., I eat my greens.

Second-person pronouns are used when someone is spoken to.

e.g., If you look, you will see your hat.

Third-person pronouns are used when a writer or speaker talks about other people and things.

e.g., They left them behind with their teacher.

Different pronouns have different jobs to do.

Personal pronouns replace the names of the people, places, animals, and everyday things around us.

- First-person pronouns are as follows:
  I, me, my, mine, us, our, ours

- Second-person pronouns are as follows:
  you, your, yours

- Third-person pronouns are as follows:
  he, his, him, she, her, hers, it, its, they, them, their, theirs

Possessive pronouns show ownership. No apostrophes are needed.

These pronouns are as follows:
my, mine, our, ours, your, yours, hers, its, their, theirs

Interrogative pronouns are used to ask certain questions—*Who? Whom?* (rarely used) *Whose? Which? What?*

e.g., Who ate all the cakes?

Whom did you see?

Whose books are on the floor?

Which bus do you catch?

What is your address?

Ideas for introducing pronouns

- Write two sentences on the board, the second containing a pronoun. Ask a student to read both.

  e.g., Brett has a new computer game. <u>He</u> got <u>it</u> for <u>his</u> birthday.

- In turn, underline *he*, *it*, and *his*, and ask what noun they refer to. Draw arrows to link *he* and *his* to *Brett*, and *it* to *computer game*.

- Add another sentence.

  e.g., <u>He</u> asked Sarah to play with <u>him</u>.

  Again use arrows to make the links back to *Brett*.

- Add another sentence.

  e.g., <u>She</u> said that <u>she</u> would like that.

  Make the links between *she* and *Sarah*.

- Introduce the term *pronoun*—a word that takes the place of a noun. Demonstrate the reasons for using pronouns instead of repeating names of people and things.

- Discuss other examples using different personal pronouns.

  e.g., *they, we, us, them, your*

- Begin a list on the side of the board.

- Hand out some simple texts and ask the students to find some more pronouns. Add any new ones to the list.

- Do some oral cloze activities, with students being able to draw answers from your list.

  e.g., Ellen read a new book. _____ liked _____ very much. _____ gave _____ to Jake to read, too.

- Hand out some storybooks. Ask the student to find some pronouns. They need to be able to say what the pronoun is and what noun it replaces.

Exploring PRONOUNS

Out of Sorts

Make enlarged copies of some different story texts. Give each student one copy. Ask the students to cut out all the different pronouns on the page. Now place the class in small groups and ask them to sort their words into categories. Some could sort them as male, female, both, or neither. Some could sort them as singular or plural. Some could sort them according to person—first, second, and third. Some could sort them between personal and possessive. The chosen texts should accommodate these choices.

Tip: You may wish to give the groups sheets of paper headed with the various categories.

Wipe-out

Select a piece of text and make an enlarged copy. White-out 10 pronouns. Make copies for each student (or pair). Ask them to write suitable pronouns in the spaces. Share answers.

In a Flash

Have pronoun flashcards prepared. Show the class a card. Ask one student to give you an oral sentence containing the pronoun.

Variation: Ask one student to give you a noun instead of the pronoun on the card that you are holding.

e.g., it—coat, she—Mrs. Tomms, they—Sue and Alan

Pick-a-Pronoun

Give each student a copy of one page of text from a storybook.

Ask them to circle or highlight all the pronouns they can find.

When finished, share their findings. This could be done in a small group or with the whole class.

Students should be able to name both the pronouns and the noun to which it refers.

As You See It

Give students a picture each from a magazine or product catalog. The pictures should include singular and plural nouns (people, places, animals, things). Ask the students to glue the picture on a sheet of paper and write some literal things about the picture. They should write at least two sentences. They should include pronouns. Demonstrate first:

e.g., Here is a girl. <u>She</u> is holding a box.
There is a dog in <u>it</u>.
e.g., There are six jars on a shelf.
<u>They</u> have jam in <u>them</u>.
<u>They</u> cost $3.50 each.

Personal Pronouns 1

A **pronoun** can take the place of a noun. (Examples: Sarah bought a new hat. <u>She</u> wears <u>it</u> to school. Janis saw Toby and Will. <u>They</u> were walking past <u>her</u> house.)

1. **Underline the pronouns in these sentences.**

   a. Please pass me the cookies.

   b. I gave him a juicy orange.

   c. She put on her pink shorts.

   d. Please give them money for the bus.

   e. We went to visit our Aunt Tilly.

Singular pronouns	Plural pronouns
I, me, my, you, your, yours, she, her, hers, he, him, his, it, its	we, us, our, ours, you, your, yours, they, them, their, theirs

2. **The pronouns are underlined. What nouns do they replace?**

   a. Ned has a pet bird. <u>He</u> (_____) keeps <u>it</u> (_____) in a cage.

   b. The cats chased the mice. <u>They</u> (_____) caught <u>them</u> (_____).

   c. Lynn bought a new hat. <u>She</u> (_____) likes wearing <u>it</u> (_____).

   d. Tom and <u>I</u> (_____) have two kittens. <u>We</u> (_____) look after <u>them</u> (_____).

   e. The children had some apples. <u>They</u> (_____) ate <u>them</u> (_____) on the bus.

3. **Replace the underlined nouns with pronouns.**

   a. <u>Selena's</u> mom gave _____ a gel pen.

   b. <u>Fred and Ella</u> like swimming. _____ go to the pool every day.

   c. <u>Jonah</u> has a pet parrot. _____ gives _____ seeds to eat.

   d. The <u>girls</u> are tired. Please wait for _____.

   e. <u>Jack</u> had a birthday. His friend gave _____ a toy car.

PRONOUNS

Personal Pronouns 2

Pronouns are used instead of nouns. *Personal pronouns* replace the names of people and things.

PRONOUNS

1. **Add pronouns so the sentences make sense.**

   a. The deer came to the water hole because _____ were thirsty.

   b. When Peter finished the book, _____ put _____ back on the shelf.

   c. Linda pushed the door. _____ jumped back when _____ opened.

   d. The children were cold, so _____ gave _____ coats.

   e. _____ have not met the teacher yet.

2. **Color the masculine (male) pronouns red.**
   Color the feminine (female) pronouns green.
   Color the plural pronouns yellow.

he	they	we	her
she	us	him	them

3. **Write three sentences. Include some of the pronouns from above.**

   _____

   _____

   _____

   _____

   _____

Possessive Pronouns 1

Possessive pronouns show ownership. No apostrophe is needed. Examples: <u>my</u> book (mine), <u>his</u> boat (his), <u>their</u> books (theirs), <u>our</u> pets (ours), <u>your</u> smile (yours), <u>her</u> dog (hers)

1. Circle the correct pronouns.

a. Dana put on (her hers) hat.

b. (Him His) friends are coming to play with (him his).

c. Is this lunch box (you yours)?

d. Give (me my) the ball. It is (my mine).

e. (They them) ate all (their theirs) lunch.

2. Add suitable pronouns from the list of possessive pronouns.

a. We went for a picnic with _____ cousins.

b. Give the book to her. It is _____.

c. They stood in line to buy _____ tickets.

d. I call _____ pet bird Fifi.

e. Tim gave _____ apple to _____ horse.

f. Did you put _____ toys away?

my	mine
your	yours
her	hers
his	
our	ours
their	theirs

PRONOUNS

3. Search for all the possessive pronouns in the list.

T	H	E	I	R	S	F	S
J	M	Y	O	U	R	L	I
I	I	O	U	R	S	G	H
M	N	U	D	A	O	U	R
H	E	R	T	H	E	I	R
Z	X	S	M	H	E	R	S

Possessive Pronouns 2

Possessive pronouns show ownership. No apostrophe is needed.
(Examples: This pencil is <u>mine</u>. That crayon is <u>yours</u>. Those paints are <u>ours</u>.)

PRONOUNS

1. Use the correct pronoun.

a. her hers	I don't know which hat is _____.
b. our ours	At _____ sports day, I won two races.
c. their theirs	Are these marbles yours or _____ ?
d. my mine	I want _____ pencil back. It is _____.

2. Beside each letter, write a suitable pronoun from the list below.

Quickly, James opened the box. *a* _____ spread Clarie's new dress on the bed. *b* _____ was very lovely. It was made of gold and silver satin. There was even a sparkling crown for *c* _____ hair. When Claire saw it, *d* _____ eyes shone. *e* _____ smiled happily. "It is the most beautiful dress *f* _____ have ever seen. Thank you, James. I shall treasure *g* _____ always," she said, and she kissed the top of *h* _____ head.

a	Him	He	It
b	She	It	They
c	his	my	her
d	her	hers	your
e	Him	She	Her
f	You	I	They
g	it	you	him
h	my	her	his

Interrogative Pronouns

Some pronouns are used to ask questions. (Examples: Who? Which? What? Whose?)

1. Answer these questions.

a. What are your favorite fruits?

_____

b. With whom do you play at lunchtime?

_____

c. Whose house is next door to yours?

_____

2. Add the correct pronoun to these sentences.

a. _____ books are on the floor?

b. _____ would you like—an apple or a peach?

c. _____ way did the ambulance go?

d. _____ is coming over to play with you?

Who
Which
Whose
What

3. Unscramble these questions. Don't forget the question mark at the end.

a. to the Who for beach their went vacation

_____

b. made Whose is brick of house

_____

c. do sport you summer play in Which the

_____

d. for night did you last What eat dinner

_____

Indefinite and Demonstrative Pronouns

Indefinite pronouns refer to people and things in a general way. (Examples: any, all, anyone, anybody, each, everyone, everybody, everything, few, many, no one, none, nothing, some, someone, something, somebody, several)

1. Add an indefinite pronoun to complete each sentence.

a. I gave _____ in my class an invitation.

b. He has six marbles, but I have _____.

c. Has _____ found my lost parrot?

d. She heard _____ calling her name.

e. There were only a _____ people left at the party.

f. We're having fruit salad. Would you like _____?

Demonstrative pronouns refer to specific people and things. The pronouns are as follows: *this* (singular), *these* (plural), *that* (singular), *those* (plural).

2. Add a demonstrative pronoun to complete each sentence.

a. "Who did _____?" Dad asked pointing to the broken window.

b. _____ was my favorite song when I was little.

c. "Put _____ back on the shelf," Mom said, handing me three books.

d. "Can I please have one of _____ big lollipops?" asked Jeremy excitedly.

e. The crane moved _____ heavy rocks, but left _____ rocks here.

f. _____ is the house that Jack built.

PRONOUNS

Assessment - Pronouns

CHECK 1: Circle the pronouns in these sentences. ☐ /10

    a. She gave him a cup of hot coffee.

    b. I went rock climbing with my four friends.

    c. They wanted to give her a big surprise.

    d. Did you know that we are going overseas?

    e. It was their uncle's birthday on Saturday.

CHECK 2: Put in the missing pronouns. ☐ /10

    Dan went to the fair with _____ brother Kade. _____ went for rides on the Ferris wheel and the merry-go-round. Then _____ saw _____ neighbor, Mrs. James, and waved to _____. Mrs. James took _____ to see all the exhibits. Afterwards, _____ said to the boys, "_____ must be hungry. Would _____ like a hamburger?"

"Thank you very much," _____ said together.

CHECK 3: Use arrows to show the nouns that the pronouns replace. ☐ /10

    a. Nuno has some silkworms. <u>He</u> keeps <u>them</u> in a shoebox.

    b. The cats chased the birds. <u>They</u> couldn't catch <u>them</u>.

    c. May-Lin bought a new dress. <u>She</u> wore <u>it</u> to the school concert.

    d. Ted and Jeff have two kittens. <u>They</u> look after <u>them</u>.

    e. Robbie and I have a puppy. <u>We</u> take <u>it</u> for walks in the park.

CHECK 4: On a separate sheet of paper, write sentences using each of these pronouns. You can use more than one pronoun in a sentence. ☐ /10

we	our	they	their	she	it	you	his	I	my

Student Name: _____

Date: _____

Total Score: _____/40

Verbs are the essential ingredient of any sentence. Without them, communication is, at best, poor. A verb gives a sentence a reason for "being." It informs of some process occurring between people and things. In the fast growing world of telecommunications, new language is being created all the time. New verbs are being born, while others are being discarded or archived. We now have, for example, the verbs *email, text, merge, autoformat.*

Verbs tie ideas together and make sense of them. They contextualize the events surrounding people, places, and things. Verbs are very powerful tools used by writers and speakers. Writers, especially, recognize the power in verbs to create strong image of movement, action, and behavior. Like adjectives, verbs give color and interest to sentences. They create vivid pictures of motion and movement; so they can be used to great effect, especially in descriptive writing and poetry.

Help students create a verb-consciousness, to build a vocabulary that is colorful and imaginative. Help them leave words like *got* behind and strive for words of color, precision and expression.

VERBS

Verbs consist of one or more words that show the particular interactions and relationships between people, places, events, and objects.

Different verbs have different jobs to do.

Doing verbs show the actions of people and things.

e.g., fly, swim, sleep, break, spill, dance, cry, wrap

Being verbs show that people and things exist.

e.g., am, is, are, was, were, be, being, been

Having verbs show what people and things "have."

e.g., has, have, having, had

Saying verbs show how living things (or personified objects) express themselves.

e.g., growl, squeak, shout, whimper, howl, whisper, say, call, cry

Verbs have different forms.

An **infinitive** is the simple verb form.

e.g., play, swim, eat, take

Finite verbs work on their own. They have someone or something as the subject.

e.g., Golden autumn leaves *fall* from the trees.
The jet plane *flew* to Paris.

Nonfinite verbs cannot work on their own. They consist of the following:

1. infinitives (e.g., I want to eat. Jani wants to play.)

2. present or past participles with an auxiliary verb (e.g., She is singing on stage. He was playing hockey. Mom has baked a roast beef dinner. Ferris had kicked the winning goal.)

The **present participle** is formed by adding *–ing* to the infinitive.

e.g., fly, flying; jump, jumping

The **past participle** is formed by adding *–ed* to the infinitive.

e.g., kick, kicked; play, played

Auxiliary (helping) verbs are used with present and past participles to make a complete verb. Their job is to show tense or possibility.

e.g., We are eating dinner. (present tense)
They were eating chips. (past tense)
I may go to Oregon next week. (possibility)

Verbs are singular or plural.

A **singular verb** is used with a singular subject.

e.g., A dog chews bones.
A cat drinks milk.

A **plural verb** is used with a plural subject.

e.g., The dogs chew bones.
The cats drink milk.

Verbs show tense.

It is the verb in a sentence that determines when something occurs. Verbs indicate three different times called *tenses.*

1. **present tense:** I am playing tennis.

2. **past tense:** Shane played soccer for South America.

3. **future tense:** They will play the final match on Saturday.

Regular/Irregular Verbs

Most verbs show tense in a regular way through the use of present or past participles.

e.g., I am dancing. (present) I danced. (past)
    He is washing his car. (present)
    He washed his car. (past)

Irregular verbs change their spelling in the past tense and the past participle.

e.g., ring, rang, rung; do, did, done

Other irregular verbs include the following: go, fly, eat, give, take, know.

Contractions

We often contract verb and (pronoun) subject.

e.g., I am = I'm; it is = it's; they are = they're

We often contract verb and negative.

e.g., will not = won't; cannot = can't;
    did not = didn't

Ideas for introducing verbs

- Play "Simon Says" with the class. After a few oral commands, say and write the verbs (infinitives) on the board (e.g., Simon says "sit," Simon says "stand," "Bow down," Simon says "wave," etc.).

- Now ask the students to imagine they are athletes. Ask them to tell you what they can do. List these words on the board (e.g., *run, swim, dive, cycle, ski, wrestle*).

- Introduce the term *verb*—a word that says what people and things do.

- Ask them now to imagine they are dogs, or cooks, or ants. List all their "doing" words on the board.

- Again talk about the term *verbs*—words used to say what people and things do.

- Write a subject on the board (e.g., boys). With the students, make a list of all the things that boys like to do, (e.g., sleep, eat, drink, jump, speak, run, sing, play, dream, skateboard).

  Write a second list of any different things girls like to do.

- Ask the student to give you a sentence (orally) about boys or girls using a listed verb. Add to the board and discuss.

- Now ask the students to give you a sentence beginning with "The boy . . ." Most students will offer a sentence where the verb has been formed by changing or adding to the *infinitive* (e.g., The boy is playing football. The boy ate the banana. The boy raced across the park.). This will give you the opportunity to speak about the verb in a sentence being one or more words and that verbs show when things happen.

- Change the subject to "The girl . . ." and explore how the verbs change.

- Write an action sentence on the board, and ask the students to identify the verb, the "doing" part of the sentence (e.g., The horse galloped past the winning post. The dog chased the cat up the tree.).

- Hand out a prepared text, which gives good examples of "doing" verbs, and ask the students to highlight the verbs.

- Ask them to list five "doing" verbs from a book they are reading. Share their lists and discuss whether the chosen words are verbs or not.

Exploring VERBS

Body Parts

Divide the class into groups of three. Give each group a sheet of paper with a simple line drawing of a person in the center. Ask the group to write as many verbs as they can around the picture.

The verbs should be only one word, and should say what a person can do with the different parts of the body (e.g., see, hear, speak, listen, taste, smell, sniff, bite, etc.).

Allow the groups two to three different sessions to prepare their verb webs to really stretch their thinking.

Each group should present their work.

The sheets of paper could be displayed on a bulletin board, or collated into a class book entitled: "Doing Verbs" or "Verbs of Action."

Ready for Action

Give one to two well-chosen storybooks to each pair of students. Ask them to skim through the pages to find and list 10 "doing" verbs. Explain that because they are storybooks, they will be written about things that have happened and many of the verbs will end in *–ed*. Demonstrate with a book of your own, writing some verbs on the board.

Out of Sorts

Give each pair of students a magazine or calendar picture, and a sheet of paper with two columns headed "NOUNS" and "VERBS." Ask each pair to write one-word nouns and one-word verbs about their picture. Stipulate between three and 10 words for each category, matching the strengths of your students.

Set a time limit of between five and eight minutes. Each pair could present their list to the class. Discuss any inaccuracies.

Variation: After three minutes, each pair passes their list on to another pair, who then adds more words. Do three or four changes before returning to the original owners for sharing.

Extension: Ask students to write two or three sentences each about their pictures, using the words they have listed to help them.

"Doing" Verbs 1

Verbs show what people and things are doing. (Examples: The bell <u>rang</u> and the children <u>walked</u> back into school. They <u>sat</u> down and <u>read</u> their books.) We often call them **"doing" verbs**.

spin
twist
throw
chop
bend
ring

roll
stand
read
buy
growl
hop

The verb is the heart of a sentence.
It brings the people and things to life by telling us what they are doing, thinking, saying, and feeling.

1. **Underline the people in these sentences. Circle what they are doing.**

   a. The farmer planted wheat in the field.

   b. The bike riders raced up the steep hill.

   c. The dancer twirls on her toes.

   d. Our class went to the museum by bus.

   e. They jump on their trampoline.

   f. The teacher counted the children in her class.

   g. I cooked sausages for breakfast.

2. **Answer these questions—"Yes" or "No."**

   a. Could you <u>lift</u> a train? _____

   b. Could you <u>carry</u> a tray of cups? _____

   c. Could you <u>send</u> an elephant through the mail? _____

   d. Should you <u>skate</u> on a road? _____

   e. Do cats and dogs <u>eat</u> wheat? _____

   f. Could you <u>fill</u> a bucket with sand? _____

   g. Have you <u>kicked</u> a goal in soccer? _____

   h. Can you <u>play</u> marbles? _____

"Doing" Verbs 2

"Doing" verbs are the words that show what people and things are doing.

1. Circle the verbs.

   a. The tennis ball bounced over the net.

   b. The phone rang, and I answered it.

   c. The teacher read us a fairy tale.

   d. Jane made her bed this morning.

   e. The plane landed on the runway.

2. Put a "doing" verb in the space and illustrate one of the sentences.

   a. The clown _____ baggy pants.

   b. He _____ the ball to his friend.

   c. Frogs are _____ in the water hole.

   d. Dad is _____ the grass.

3. Can you say what these people and things do?

   a. Dogs _____ their tails.

   b. Fish _____ in the sea.

   c. Lions _____ for food.

   d. People _____ golf.

   e. Hens _____ eggs.

   f. We _____ our hands.

   g. Artists _____ pictures.

   h. Rain _____ on rooftops.

   i. Children _____ kites.

   j. We _____ our teeth.

   k. People _____ cars.

   l. Boys and girls _____ bikes.

VERBS

"Saying" Verbs

Verbs show how people express their feelings. (Examples: Mary <u>mumbled</u>. Stella <u>stuttered</u>. Graham <u>grumbled</u>.) We often call them "saying" verbs.

1. Choose a word from the list to complete each sentence.

talk	cried	ask
gasped	say	explained

a. Did you _____ your mother if you could come over to play?

b. I can't hear you. What did you _____?

c. I will _____ with you on the phone tonight.

d. Mrs. Jugg _____ how she made pancakes.

e. Susan _____ when she missed the bus.

f. Molly _____ when she saw her birthday surprise.

2. Write sentences using these verbs.

giggles _____

shouted _____

told _____

sighed _____

3. Use a better word than *said* in these sentences.

a. "You must never do that again," said their mother.   _____

b. "I always get my spelling right," said Meg.   _____

c. Beth said to her friend, "Tell me the answer."   _____

d. "Get out of my way!" said the angry driver.   _____

VERBS

"Being" and "Having" Verbs 1

The words *has*, *have*, and *had* are used as verbs.

They work on their own.
He <u>has</u> ten dollars.
I <u>have</u> a new bike.
She <u>had</u> no lunch.

They also help other verbs.
He <u>has done</u> his homework.
I <u>have written</u> a story.
She <u>had seen</u> the movie.

1. Use *has*, *have*, and *had* to complete the sentences.

a. _____ you been here before?

b. Mrs. Jones _____ planted rose bushes in her garden.

c. We _____ baby birds in our yard.

d. They _____ lived in Los Angeles for six years.

e. I was sure that he _____ missed the plane.

f. The two boys _____ spent all their money.

g. Did you _____ eggs and toast for breakfast?

h. Amanda _____ wide blue eyes.

The word *be* is used as a verb. The **"being" verbs** are as follows: *am, is, are, was, were, *be, *being, *been.*

be, being, and *been* are only used with other verbs.

2. Choose "being" verbs to fill the blanks.

a. I _____ seven years old.

b. They _____ all in my class.

c. He _____ with Kyle yesterday.

d. We have _____ here before.

e. Nathan _____ first in the line.

f. I will _____ eight in July.

g. We _____ home last night.

h. She _____ older than I am.

i. You are _____ silly!

j. Where have you _____?

"Being" and "Having" Verbs 2

The words *has, have, had* and *be* are used as verbs. The **"being" verbs** are as follows: *am, is, are, was, were* and *be, being, been,* which are only used with other verbs.

1. Circle the verbs.

a. The soldier has a rifle over his shoulder.

b. We each had two jelly beans.

c. She is five, and her sister is eight.

d. The bus was early, but the children were already there.

e. I am sure they are not upstairs.

2. Use a "being" or "having" verb in the space. Could you have chosen a different one? Write it in the parentheses.

a. They _____ in the park. (_____)

b. She _____ my new friend. (_____)

c. The girls _____ ribbons in their hair. (_____)

d. Only one book _____ on the table. (_____)

3. Write in the blank the missing words. Use the words in the box to help you.

writing	eaten	been	waiting	running

a. My dog has _____ his bone.

b. Were you _____ for me to come?

c. Everyone in our class is _____ a poem.

d. They had never _____ in a helicopter before.

e. Soon we will be _____ in the cross-country race.

VERBS

"Helping" Verbs

Some verbs help other verbs do their work. **Helping verbs** tell us <u>when</u> something is happening.

Here are some examples:

The dog <u>is chasing</u> the cat. *(now)*
We <u>will eat</u> dinner at seven o'clock. *(future)*
They <u>have bought</u> their tickets. *(past)*
We <u>might be going</u> to the zoo. *(possible future)*

Meet the Helpers!

am   is   are
was   were
do   did
has   have
had
shall   will
can
must   may
might
could   would
should

1. Use a helping verb to complete these sentences.

a. Jack and Jill _____ going up the hill.

b. James _____ bought a new baseball bat.

c. I _____ come with you to the supermarket.

d. _____ you enjoy our vacation?

e. I _____ ask my mom if I _____ go.

2. Add a suitable "doing" verb.

a. They will _____ a letter to Aunt May.

b. If I could _____, I would jump into the pool.

c. We have _____ our bus tickets.

d. He is _____ on top of the ladder.

e. Can you _____ over that brick wall?

3. Write sentences using these verb phrases.

was playing   *can fly*   *has cooked*

_____

_____

_____

VERBS

Negative with Verbs

We use the word *not* to say something negative. (Examples: He is <u>not</u> happy. They were <u>not</u> late. I am <u>not</u> very tall. We are <u>not</u> ready.)

1. Complete these negative sentences.

a. I will not _____

b. Mom does not have _____

c. We are not _____

d. The goat would not _____

e. The team may not _____

2. Rewrite the sentences in negative form by using *not*.

a. Mr. Jones does have a new car.

_____

b. The miner has gone down into the coal mine.

_____

c. We are going to the beach.

_____

d. I can come with you tomorrow.

_____

e. She was swimming in the lake.

_____

3. Design a poster. Choose one.

- Do not fish in the lake.
- Do not enter this room.
- Do not play with matches.
- Do not write on walls.

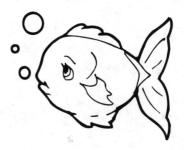

VERBS

Verbs - Contractions 1

Sometimes, the helper and *not* combine to make one word. This word is called a **contraction**. (Examples: do not = don't, has not = hasn't, could not = couldn't)

1. Match and color the contractions with the words they replace. Use a different color for each contraction.

doesn't	had not	didn't	would not	haven't	do not
won't	were not	wouldn't	was not	aren't	have not
hadn't	does not	can't	cannot	don't	could not
weren't	will not	wasn't	did not	couldn't	are not

2. Underline the contractions. Write the words they replace in parentheses.

    a. He said he <u>wouldn't</u> be home late.   (_____**would not**_____)

    b. It hasn't rained for weeks.   (_____)

    c. Why didn't you eat your lunch?   (_____)

    d. There weren't any tickets left for the game. (_____)

    e. Do you know why we haven't been called? (_____)

3. Rewrite these sentences in negative form using contractions.

    a. Sam could swim very well.   _____

    b. We will be singing in the choir. _____

    c. They have bought a pizza.   _____

    d. Her hair has been cut.   _____

    e. Jilly is playing hockey today.   _____

VERBS

Singular and Plural Verbs

Verbs are "doing" words. The subject of the sentence tells us who, or what, is involved in the "doing." The verb ties the subject to the rest of the sentence.

The SUBJECT

| The big black dog | | chased the cat up the tree. |

1. What is the subject of these sentences?

   a. The children hurried out to play cricket.   The children

   b. We are going for a picnic tomorrow. _____

   c. Many of my friends ride bikes to school. _____

   d. A soft gray koala is nibbling gum leaves. _____

   e. Ben and I joined a junior soccer club. _____

A singular subject has a singular verb. (Example: The horse <u>lives</u> on a farm.)
A plural subject has a plural verb. (Example: The horses <u>live</u> on a farm.)
A verb and its subject always agree in number.

VERBS

2. Write these statements in plural form.

Singular number *(one)*	**Plural number (more than one)**
a. The snake slides.	The snakes slide.
b. The bird sings.	_____
c. The door is open.	_____
d. The boy has freckles.	_____
e. My cat likes milk.	_____
f. The dog was barking.	_____
g. She walks to school.	_____
h. I am hungry.	_____

Verbs – Contractions 2

Many subjects and verbs are written as contractions. (Examples: she will = she'll, I would = I'd, we have = we've, they are = they're)

Usually, a pronoun subject and a helping verb contract to one word.
(Example: *he is* becomes *he's*)

An apostrophe marks the spot!

1. Match and color the contractions with the words they replace. Use a different color for each contraction.

I'll	they have	I'm	it is	I've	we will
he's	you have	you're	we have	you'll	they would
they've	I will	they're	you are	he'd	you will
we're	she would	it's	he will	she's	I have
she'd	he is	he'll	they are	they'd	he would
you've	we are	we've	I am	we'll	she is

2. Circle the correct word in parentheses.

a. (Your You're) not afraid of the dark, are you?

b. (We're Were) going to the beach on Sunday.

c. The bird flew back to (its it's) nest.

d. (There They're) too busy to come tonight.

Verbs – Contractions 3

A pronoun subject and a helping verb often contract to one word.

1. Circle the contractions. Write the two words in full.

a. They've been playing football. (__They have__)

b. Do you know where he's going? (_____)

c. They'll know why it's so important. (_____) (_____)

d. I'm so glad that you're feeling better. (_____) (_____)

e. He'll be pleased to hear they're back. (_____) (_____)

f. You'll never guess what we've found! (_____) (_____)

Other pronouns that contract are as follows: *who, what, that.*

2. Find the contractions. Write the two words in full.

a. Who's knocking on the door? (__Who is__)

b. What's the answer to my question? (_____)

c. I'm not sure that's the answer. (_____) (_____)

d. Who's been sleeping in my bed? (_____)

VERBS

Verbs - Tense

Verbs tell <u>when</u> things are happening.

Present tense	now	*I jump.*
Past tense	in the past	*I jumped.*
Future tense	in the future	*I will jump.*

1. Say whether the verbs show *past*, *present*, or *future* tense.

a. Yesterday, we <u>went</u> for a swim in the dam. _____

b. The children <u>are building</u> sandcastles. _____

c. The men <u>will ride</u> across the desert on camels. _____

d. Can you see who <u>is coming</u> down the street? _____

e. I <u>saw</u> the baby panda bear at the zoo. _____

f. I <u>will wait</u> here until you have finished your work. _____

2. Draw these *present* tense happenings.

SINGULAR		
He <u>is skateboarding</u>.	I <u>am riding</u> my bike.	Mom <u>is sweeping</u>.

PLURAL		
The cars <u>are racing</u>.	Lights <u>are flashing</u>.	Children <u>are reading</u>.

VERBS

Verbs - Present Tense

Many present tense verbs are formed by adding *–ing*. (Examples: cook = cooking, like = liking, hop = hopping)
They always need a helper. (Examples: We <u>are going</u>. They <u>were hopping</u>.)

1. Add *–ing* to these base verbs. Remember your spelling rules. The spelling of some words may change when adding *–ing*.

cook	cooking	like	liking	hop	hopping
a. puff	_____	*f.* chase	_____	*k.* stop	_____
b. read	_____	*g.* bounce	_____	*l.* chat	_____
c. teach	_____	*h.* ride	_____	*m.* tug	_____
d. roll	_____	*i.* leave	_____	*n.* nod	_____
e. bleed	_____	*j.* slide	_____	*o.* grip	_____

2. Add a subject to these present tense sentences.

a. _____ are playing touch football.

b. _____ is protecting its babies from enemies.

c. _____ are galloping around the show ground.

d. _____ am writing a story about a black cat.

e. _____ are drinking hot chocolate.

3. Complete these sentences in the present tense.

a. We are reading _____

b. Tom is hoping _____

c. Lily is cooking _____

d. I am learning _____

e. They are watching _____

Verbs – Past Tense

Many past tense verbs are formed by adding –ed.
(Examples: cook = cooked, hop = hopped,
like = liked)

1. **Write the past tense of these verbs. Remember your spelling rules. The spelling of some words may change when adding –ed.**

cook	cooked	like	liked	hop	hopped
a. help _____		**f.** share _____		**k.** plan _____	
b. rain _____		**g.** close _____		**l.** stop _____	
c. start _____		**h.** change _____		**m.** pin _____	
d. watch _____		**i.** live _____		**n.** rob _____	
e. call _____		**j.** fade _____		**o.** grin _____	

2. **Complete these sentences. Choose words from the list above.**

   a. It _____ to rain, so we went home.

   b. A crowd of people _____ the house fire.

   c. At the show, we _____ a bag of popcorn.

   d. We _____ Jackson, but he never came.

   e. The police _____ the men who had _____ the bank.

Some verbs are quite irregular in the past tense. Look at the examples.
I ring the bell.   I go to school.   They come here often
I <u>rang</u> the bell.   I <u>went</u> to school.   They <u>came</u> here often.

3. **Write the past tense of these verbs.**

   a. eat _____   **e.** is _____   **i.** run _____

   b. give _____   **f.** sing _____   **j.** has _____

   c. spend _____   **g.** grow _____   **k.** stand _____

   d. dig _____   **h.** do _____   **l.** break _____

Verbs - Future Tense

Future tense tells us about things to come. The helping verbs <u>will</u> or <u>shall</u> are usually needed to show future tense.

1. Write sentences to tell of future events. Here are some starters.

  a. Tomorrow _____

  b. Next week _____

  c. This afternoon _____

  d. When I grow up _____

  Go back and circle your verbs. These verbs show future tense.

2. Draw a picture to complete the sentence.

  a. Neil <u>will eat</u> the _____ .

  b. We <u>shall buy</u> some _____ .

  c. I <u>will light</u> the _____ .

  d. We <u>will</u> soon <u>have</u> a pet _____ .

3. Read the sentences. Underneath each one, write *past*, *present*, or *future*.

a. We went bowling last night.	*d.* I will wash my hands before dinner.	*g.* The fishermen caught many fish in their nets.
_____	_____	_____
b. Ganesh and I are playing marbles.	*e.* Josh was chosen for the football team.	*h.* I am learning to play the piano.
_____	_____	_____
c. I will send a birthday card to my friend.	*f.* Alex is preparing a talk about snakes.	*i.* We will cross the harbor by ferry.
_____	_____	_____

VERBS

Assessment--Verbs

CHECK 1: Circle all the verbs in this text. □ /5

   a. Molly saved enough money for a fluffy coat.

   b. Selena was holding a basket of bread over her arm.

   c. Come with me, please.

   d. The boats have drifted away from the riverbank.

   e. I will see my grandma in just a few more days.

**CHECK 2: Write the contraction of the underlined words
in the parentheses.** □ /5

   a. We <u>could not</u> cross the deep river. (_____)

   b. <u>He is</u> writing a story about a clumsy frog. (_____)

   c. <u>What is</u> your name? (_____)

   d. <u>Did</u> you <u>not</u> see where you were going? (_____)

   e. <u>You are</u> just in time for tea. (_____)

CHECK 3: Circle the correct verb. □ /5

   a. My feet (is are) cold in winter.

   b. They didn't know who we (was were).

   c. I (is am) going for a ride in a big truck.

   d. You (are is) too late!

   e. Who (was were) all those people?

CHECK 4: Write these verbs in the past tense. □ /5

   a. grow   **b.** carry   **c.** hop   **d.** shake   **e.** is

_____   _____   _____   _____   _____

VERBS

Assessment--Verbs

CHECK 5: Use the correct word—*saw* or *seen*. ☐ /5

    a. We _____ him playing ice hockey.

    b. They have already _____ the movie twice.

    c. I _____ her waiting at the bus stop.

    d. The miner has _____ a light in the tunnel.

    e. The travelers had not _____ snow before.

CHECK 6: Choose the correct verb. ☐ /5

    a. A snail (moves move) very slowly.

    b. Rats (chew chews) through paper and rope.

    c. The boys (has have) freckles.

    d. Everyone (try tries) to come first in a race.

    e. The men (drives drive) very fast on the race track.

CHECK 7: Complete by using different "saying" verbs. ☐ /5

    a. "Why are you so late?" _____ Dad, angrily.

    b. Peta _____, "I left my backpack on the bus."

    c. "Please, please, don't tell anyone," _____ Jody.

    d. "Can't you see I'm busy," _____ her father.

    e. Owen _____, "I've left my hat at home again!"

CHECK 8: Circle the incorrect word. Write the correct word. ☐ /5

    a. Jack done all his homework. _____

    b. What have you did with all my marbles? _____

    c. They could not have did that without you. _____

    d. He asked Chen what he done for a living. _____

    e. Have you did as you were told? _____

VERBS

Student Name: _____

Date: _____

Total Score: _____/40

Adverbs are the words that add meaning to the actions of people, places, events, and objects. They tell us how, when, and where things happen.

Nouns give the things around us names, adjectives give them faces, and verbs give them something to do or say.

Adverbs are the words that create the context of those actions.

They tell us about the movements, mood, mannerisms, and body language of the people or objects involved.

They tell us about the times and the places where events occur.

Adverbs add meaning to:

- a verb (e.g., He runs <u>fast</u>.)

- an adjective (e.g., He is a <u>very</u> fast runner.)

- another adverb (e.g., He runs <u>too</u> fast for me.)

Different adverbs have different jobs to do.

Adverbs of manner tell how something is done.

e.g., He nodded <u>anxiously</u>. She spoke <u>slowly</u>.

Many adverbs of manner end in –*ly*.

e.g., quickly, lazily, fiercely, silently, busily, angrily, warily

NOTE: A few words ending in –*ly* are adjectives.

e.g., surly man, early bird, curly hair

It is easy to spot the adverb. They add meaning to verbs, adjectives, and other adverbs—NEVER to nouns.

Adverbs of time tell when things happen.

e.g., yesterday, tomorrow, long ago, next week, on Tuesday, now

Adverbs of time also tell how often things happen.

e.g., often, seldom, usually, occasionally, once, twice, daily

Adverbs of place tell where things are happening.

e.g., here, there, everywhere, somewhere, away, around, over

Interrogative adverbs are used to ask certain questions.

e.g., <u>How</u> are you? <u>Where</u> did you come from? <u>Why</u> have you come? <u>When</u> will you go?

Adverbs of degree show the extent to which something happens.

e.g., very, almost, nearly, scarcely, completely, absolutely

Adverbs, like adjectives, also have three forms:

- positive degree
  e.g., The plane flew <u>high</u>.

- comparative degree
  e.g., Another plane flew <u>higher</u>.

- superlative degree
  e.g., Jason's plane flew <u>highest</u>.

Generally, we add –*er* or –*est* to adverbs of one syllable.

e.g., high, higher, highest; hard, harder, hardest

Thus, some adverbs of degree will look like adjectives. Always remember that adverbs add meaning to verbs, adjectives, and other adverbs—NEVER to nouns.

Adverbs ending in –*ly* have *more* or *most* before them to show degree.

e.g., silently, more silently, most silently

Ideas for introducing adverbs

- Ask the students to think about all the things boys and girls can do. Give them some oral examples: they can run, skip, jump, climb.

- Brainstorm and list any number of words on the board.

- Select a verb to work with, and write a sentence on the board. (e.g., The girls skip.)

- Have a brainstorming session with the class— ask the students to suggest some words that tell us <u>how</u> the girls are skipping. List these under the heading "How." Ask different students to read the new sentences.

  e.g., The girls skip   <u>quickly</u>.

                      <u>slowly</u>

                      <u>skillfully</u>

                      <u>happily</u>

                      <u>well</u>

- Introduce the word *adverb*—a word we use to tell us <u>how</u> the girls are skipping.

- Together make a list of words that might tell us <u>how</u> someone does something.

- Repeat this process with a different sentence. (e.g., The boys run.)

- Ask the students to choose a verb from the list and write a short sentence, adding an adverb that tells how (manner).

- Write a number of these sentences on the board for discussion and comment.

- Together write a definition of an adverb. An adverb is one word that tells us <u>how</u> something happens.

- Go back to the original sentence and, this time, ask the students to say <u>when</u> the girls might be skipping. Write their responses on the board. The sentence will change tense with different suggestions.

e.g., The girls skipped yesterday. The girls will skip tomorrow. The girls skip often/sometimes.

- Again introduce the word *adverb*—a word we use to tell us <u>when</u> the girls are skipping.

- Together make a list of words that might tell us <u>when</u> someone does something.

- Again ask the students to choose a verb from the list and write a sentence, adding an adverb of time.

- Write a number of these sentences on the board for discussion and comment.

- Add to your definition of an adverb. Adverbs are words that tell us <u>how</u> and <u>when</u> something happens.

- Explain that adverbs also tell us <u>where</u> something happens. Illustrate with sentences like the following:

The boys run backwards. The boys run away. The boys run here and there.

- Together make a list of words that might tell us where someone does something.

- Add the final part of your definition: adverbs are words that tell us <u>how</u>, <u>when</u>, and <u>where</u> something happens (adverbs of manner, time, and place).

- Ask students to choose a verb from the list and write one sentence. They should include one adverb that tells how, when, or where. Share what they have written, discuss, and answer any questions.

Note: Students will probably offer adverbial phrases as responses. Acknowledge these, but don't record them here.

Exploring ADVERBS

Gradverbs (Great Adverbs)

Many stories include adverbs of manner. Many of these adverbs end in –*ly*. Select a range of suitable storybooks to illustrate this. Give each student one book, and ask them to scan through the pages and list any words that end in –*ly*—one per slip of paper. Give them a time limit of about eight minutes. When they are finished, place the students in small groups and ask them to glue their words on a sheet of paper with the heading "Adverbs that tell HOW." When completed, ask each group to present and display their work. Explore their understanding of adverbs.

Extension: Next time, also ask the students to list the verbs that the adverbs say more about.

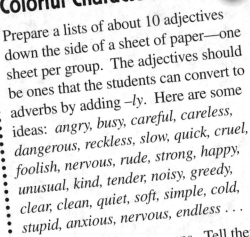

Colorful Characters

Prepare a lists of about 10 adjectives down the side of a sheet of paper—one sheet per group. The adjectives should be ones that the students can convert to adverbs by adding –*ly*. Here are some ideas: *angry, busy, careful, careless, dangerous, reckless, slow, quick, cruel, foolish, nervous, rude, strong, happy, unusual, kind, tender, noisy, greedy, clear, clean, quiet, soft, simple, cold, stupid, anxious, nervous, endless . . .*

Place the students in groups. Tell them that their job is to change the adjectives to adverbs, by adding –*ly*.

Before starting, review the spelling rule for words ending in *y*. When the groups have completed their lists, share and discuss. Reinforce that adjectives add meaning to nouns, and adverbs add meaning to verbs.

At the Starting Gate

Prepare a number of sheets of paper with a sentence "starter" at the top of each one. (e.g., Jack walked . . . , Sarah danced . . . , Boys played . . . , The man drove . . . , Ants move . . . , The children ate . . . .)

Divide the class into groups of three or four, and give each group one of the "starters" and a black marker. First, demonstrate how to write a list of adverbs around a starter on the board. Include adverbs that tell HOW, WHEN, and WHERE. Allow students five minutes to list as many adverbs as they can about their starter. Then they pass their sheet onto the next group. Each group should try to add some more adverbs. Allow about three minutes. Return the sheets to the original owners. Invite the groups to present their work, in turn. Discuss the results—are the words adverbs? What do they tell us?

Adverbs – Manner, Time, Place 1

An **adverb** is a word that tells us more about the verb. (Examples: The dog barked <u>loudly</u>. I'll be back <u>tomorrow</u>. Wait <u>here</u> for me. Let's go home <u>now</u>.)

HOW

Jeff ran <u>quickly</u>.

WHEN

Jeff ran <u>yesterday</u>.

WHERE

Jeff ran <u>away</u>.

1. **The adverb in each sentence is underlined. Does it say HOW or WHEN or WHERE about the verb?**

   a. A bird sang <u>softly</u> outside my window. _____

   b. We are going to the beach <u>soon</u>. _____

   c. The seagull is flying <u>high</u>. _____

   d. We <u>sometimes</u> play tag. _____

   e. "You all sang <u>well</u>," said the teacher. _____

2. **Underline the adverbs in each sentence. Remember adverbs tell HOW, WHEN, and WHERE.**

   a. A seagull squawked loudly in the sky.

   b. Millie is six-years-old today.

   c. She spoke quietly to her baby sister.

   d. Your book is here on this table.

   e. You go now and I'll come later.

   f. The horse galloped away.

3. **On a separate sheet of paper, use these adverbs in sentences—*often, slowly, somewhere*.**

ADVERBS

Adverbs - Manner, Time, Place 2

An **adverb** is a word that tells us more about the verb. Adverbs tell us <u>how</u>, <u>when</u>, and <u>where</u> something happens.

1. Add an adverb to each sentence. The words below will help you.

here	*backwards*	*high*	*yesterday*
quietly	*often*	*wearily*	*once*
there	*quickly*	*sometimes*	*loudly*

a. A rooster crowed _____. *(how?)*

b. I went to a barbeque _____. *(when?)*

c. Toby is waiting _____. *(where?)*

d. The old man stood up _____. *(how?)*

e. Bella dived _____ into the pool. *(how?)*

f. He _____ goes fishing. *(when?)*

2. Search out the adverbs.

everywhere

often

sometimes

outside

today

down

forwards

later

high

away

D	T	Y	E	N	T	O	D	A	Y
O	F	S	G	J	U	B	K	L	A
W	G	E	D	I	S	T	U	O	W
N	P	M	V	D	D	H	J	R	A
Q	H	I	X	L	R	G	K	Z	I
L	A	T	E	R	A	I	N	P	F
E	V	E	R	Y	W	H	E	R	E
K	O	M	W	E	R	Y	N	C	B
H	U	O	J	D	O	F	T	E	N
T	R	S	N	U	F	L	Y	Z	B

ADVERBS

Adverbs 1

Adjectives add meaning to nouns.
Adverbs add meaning to verbs.

1. **Silly Sam has written the wrong adverbs. Can you help him correct them? Cross out the wrong word and write the correct adverb on the line.**

   a. The horse ran slowly and won the race.   _____

   b. Jamie spoke softly, and everyone heard him.   _____

   c. We will go trail bike riding yesterday.   _____

   d. The man went up the ladder to the ground.   _____

   e. A compass needle points south.   _____

2. **Join the sentence parts together.**

a. He crept	hard	for many days.
b. I spoke	early	up the stairs.
c. He pushed	silently	so everyone could hear.
d. She arrived	north	and the door opened.
e. It rained	loudly	from Miami.
f. They traveled	heavily	and had to wait.

3. **Use these adverbs in sentences of your own.**

   accidentally _____

   _____

   outside _____

   _____

   tonight _____

   _____

ADVERBS

Adverbs 2

Many adverbs are formed by adding –ly to the adjective. (Examples: slow—slowly, quick—quickly, smooth—smoothly, cold—coldly)

1. Here is a list of adjectives and adverbs. Fill in the blanks.

Adjective	Adverb	Adjective	Adverb
a. clear	clearly	**f.** excited	
b.	sweetly	**g.** foolish	
c. dangerous		**h.**	carefully
d.	silently	**i.**	kindly
e. simple		**j.** busy	

2. Circle the correct word in the parentheses.

a. Ssh! You are speaking too (loud loudly).

b. The doctor nodded his head (wise wisely).

c. He did the work (bad badly).

d. That homework was very (simple simply).

e. Please stand (quiet quietly) beside your sister.

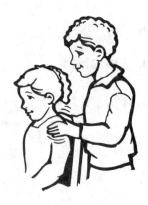

3. Complete the sentences by using adverbs. Make the adverbs by adding –ly to an adjective in the box.

a. Jack hurried off _____ to catch the train.

b. She smiled _____ and opened her gift.

c. The pigs _____ ate the corn mash.

d. The children rushed _____ out to play.

e. Mr. Jones shook his fist _____ .

angry
greedy
happy
noisy
hasty

Interrogative Adverbs

Some adverbs are used to ask questions. How? When? Where? Why?

Examples: <u>Why</u> are you shouting?
<u>How</u> do you make pancakes?
<u>When</u> are you going to visit me?
<u>Where</u> did you go for your vacation?

1. Choose the correct adverb to complete these questions.

a. _____ did you go fishing?

b. _____ is she looking so sad?

c. _____ do you make chocolate cookies?

d. _____ will the train arrive from New York?

e. _____ must you leave so soon?

f. _____ far is it to the skating rink?

2. Answer these questions.

a. When is your birthday? _____

b. How old will you be? _____

c. Where do you go to school? _____

d. When do you get home from school? _____

e. Where do you play with your friends? _____

3. Unscramble these questions. Remember to use question marks.

a. the Why are laughing children _____

b. is football the When final game _____

c. bike like you How your do new _____

d. rabbit can Where pet I a buy _____

ADVERBS

Assessment - Adverbs

CHECK 1: **The adverbs have been underlined. Do they say HOW or WHEN or WHERE about the verbs?** ☐ /6

a. Come <u>here</u> and sit with me. _____

b. The sun will be setting <u>soon</u>. _____

c. A crab walks <u>sideways</u>. _____

d. Let's go bike riding <u>tomorrow</u>. _____

e. I am going <u>inside</u> for dinner. _____

f. Speak as <u>quietly</u> as you can. _____

CHECK 2: **Circle five adverbs in this story.** ☐ /5

Emma and John climbed steadily up the mountain trail. They had left home early in the morning in thick fog. The sun shone brightly, and they felt warm and dry. Soon they would reach the halfway mark. There they would rest awhile.

CHECK 3: **Change these adjectives to adverbs.** ☐ /10

a. happy _____   **f.** weak _____

b. steep _____   **g.** strong _____

c. hungry _____   **h.** thick _____

d. lazy _____   **i.** slow _____

e. loose _____   **j.** easy _____

CHECK 4: **Complete these questions that you might ask your friend.** ☐ /4

a. When _____

b. How _____

c. Where _____

d. Why _____

CHECK 5: **The adverbs have been underlined.**
Circle the verbs they say more about. ☐ /5

a. He opened one eye <u>sleepily</u>.

b. I <u>often</u> play the piano.

c. He turned the bucket <u>upside down</u>.

d. The farmer looked <u>anxiously</u> at the sky.

e. Now it is raining <u>heavily</u>.

CHECK 6: **Circle the correct word in the parentheses.** ☐ /5

a. The lady spoke (gentle gently) to us.

b. "I am (proud proudly) of you," said our coach.

c. He bought the apples (cheap cheaply) at the market.

d. (Careful Carefully) she tied the rope to a tree.

e. I am a (strong strongly) swimmer.

CHECK 7: **Join the sentence parts correctly.** ☐ /5

a. We went	away	around the hive.
b. Bees buzzed	brightly	and broke.
c. The cup fell	outside	in the blue sky.
d. The bird flew	noisily	to play in our tree house.
e. The sun shone	down	into a tall tree.

ADVERBS

Student Name: _____

Date: _____   Total Score: _____/40

A sentence is a meaningful chunk of language.

It contains a complete idea.

Sentences are the building blocks of our language, and it is through our spoken and written language that we understand each other and the world.

It is through language that we interact with each other, statement by statement, question by answer, request by response.

We have a vast array of words to choose from, to enable us to give our utterances precise, unambiguous meaning.

We have a whole range of techniques that enable us to manipulate our language.

We can inspire and uplift our audience and move them to laughter or tears.

Language gives us the power to control the many situations that arise in our life.

SENTENCES

A sentence is a chunk of language, which must have at least one verb, and make sense. In written English it is bound by a capital letter and a period, question mark, or exclamation mark.

A baby deer bounded across the snow.

When the curtain went up, everyone stopped talking.

Statements relate facts (or opinions) and are bound by a capital letter and a period.

e.g., He is entering college this year. There are thirty students in my class. Uniforms should be worn in all schools. The moon landing was the greatest event in history.

Questions ask questions and expect answers. They are bound by a capital letter and a question mark.

* They can begin with an interrogative adjective, adverb, or pronoun.

e.g., Where did you find my keys? Whose are these? Which shirt do you like? Why didn't you wait?

* They can be written as a statement with a question on the end.

e.g., You will buy a ticket, won't you? They went swimming yesterday, didn't they?

Exclamations stress the importance of the words in the sentence. They are bound by a capital letter and an exclamation mark.

e.g., What! You forgot your money! I'm going now, and I'm not coming back!

Commands request or demand an action from the listener or reader. They are bound by a capital letter and a period or exclamation mark. Commands usually begin with a verb in the present tense.

e.g., Cut out all the pictures on the page. Don't forget to bring a raincoat. Open the door and switch on the light, please. Get out! And don't come back!

Sentences are structured in different ways.

Simple sentences have two parts—a subject and a predicate, which contains the verb.

| *Little Bo-Peep* | *lost her sheep.* |

Compound sentences consist of two simple sentences joined by a coordinate conjunction—*and, but, so, for, nor, yet, or.*

e.g., Jake drove the car <u>and</u> Mary read the map. I'd like to go to the football game, <u>but</u> I don't have a ticket. Jane is coming over, <u>so</u> we can play chess. Would you like to read, <u>or</u> do you want to play outside?

Punctuation of Sentences

Capital letters are used:

* for the first word in a sentence.
  e.g., There's a hole in my pocket.
* for proper nouns within sentences.
  e.g., She handed Mr. Jazz his ticket to New York.
* for the first spoken word in dialogue.
  e.g., Jim said, "My mom bought a rug at the market." His brother added, "And a little brown teapot."
* to emphasize words in a sentence.
  e.g., You're SO bossy.
  You did WHAT?

Periods end statements and commands.

e.g., The waterfall was spectacular. Close the gate behind you.

Question marks end questions.

e.g., I'm thirsty, aren't you? Do you want a can of
    root beer?

Exclamation marks end exclamations.

e.g., Trust Eddie to forget! What a surprise!

Commas are used:

* to separate words in a list.
    e.g., At the fruit stand, I bought apples, pears,
        bananas, figs, and watermelon.

* to separate a beginning phrase or clause from the
    rest of the sentence.
    e.g., Late that afternoon, we arrived home from
        our long trip. Although we were tired, we
        unpacked the car.

* to separate an embedded phrase or clause from
    the rest of the sentence.
    e.g., Aunt Jean, wearing her purple hat, drove off
        to the shops. The storm, which we had been
        promised, did not happen.

* to separate spoken from unspoken words in
    dialogue.
    e.g., "This is the house I once lived in," sighed
        Madison.
        "It must have been fun," said Sue, "to sleep
        up in that attic room."

Quotation marks are used around spoken words in
dialogue.

e.g., "Dinner is at seven o'clock," called Dad.
    Jo whispered, "What do you think we're having?"

Apostrophes are used:

* with nouns to show possession. e.g., <u>Jack's</u> clothes

* to contract pronouns and helping verbs. e.g., <u>We've</u>
    packed a picnic lunch. <u>You're</u> invited to come.

* to contract helping verbs and negatives. e.g., I
    <u>can't</u> sleep. Ben <u>didn't</u> win. She <u>wasn't</u> lost.

Person

Sentences can be written from three different points of
view.

* **First-person** point of view is when a writer,
    speaker, or character is doing the "talking."
    e.g., <u>I</u> eat my greens. These CDs are <u>mine</u>.

* **Second-person** point of view is used when
    someone is spoken to.
    e.g., If <u>you</u> look, <u>you</u> will see <u>your</u> hat.

* **Third-person** point of view is used when writers
    and speakers talk about other people and things.
    e.g., <u>They</u> were left behind with <u>their</u> teacher.

Ideas for introducing sentences

* Write a great, descriptive verb on the board.
    (e.g., crash)

* Ask the students what they think about when
    they see that word. Pick up on a topic from the
    answers they give you and write it on the board.
    (e.g., truck)

* Ask them how we might say something about
    the truck and the crash. They will probably
    respond in sentences. Write some of these on
    the board:

    e.g., The truck crashed into a tree.
        The truck was going too fast and crashed.
        A truck and a car crashed.
        The truck crashed and the driver was hurt.

* Tell the students that there are four ideas about
    a truck and a crash. Each idea is called a
    <u>sentence</u>.

* Repeat this process with another word.
    (e.g., melt) Again talk about the concept of
    a sentence being one idea. Point out that a
    sentence begins with a capital letter and ends
    with a period. This "fences in" the idea. We
    can tell where it starts and where it ends.

* Write another colorful verb (e.g., squeeze) on
    the board. This time list a number of topic
    words (such as oranges, hand, toothpaste, hole
    in the wall) and ask students to pick one and
    think of one idea for a sentence. Write several
    responses on the board.

* Ask the students about their understanding of
    a sentence.

* Write two more great verbs on the board, and
    ask students to write a sentence for each.

* Share, discuss, and reflect on their learning.

* Return to this process at a later date, to extend
    their learning by introducing the work of
    adjectives or adverbs.

Exploring SENTENCES

The Great Sentence Search

Remind your students that we are surrounded by sentences every day—in newspapers, catalogs, magazines, TV guides, advertising slogans, storybooks, comics, billboards. Send your students on "The Great Sentence Search." Ask them to jot down any sentences that appeal to them. How do they know a sentence? It is "fenced in" with a capital letter and a period (or perhaps a ? or a !). Ask them to record their sentences on strips of paper, as many as they can, and "mail" them in a special "The Great Sentence Search" box. They have two days!

Note: Advise the students that their sentences must be written well, so they can be read easily. Set aside a time for sharing "The Great Sentence Search" strips. Use this opportunity to consolidate the concept of a sentence as one idea, "fenced in" by a capital letter and a period.

In the Bag

Cut out photos from a newspaper or magazine, six for every pair of students. Write a sentence about each one. Store the sentences and photos in a plastic, zipper bag. Give each pair of students a bag, and ask them to match the sentences and photos. Pairs should take turns to read the matched sentences to each other. Sentences and photos are then returned to their bag for reuse.

Heads and Tails

Prepare some simple sentence strips, large enough for the students to handle easily. Cut the sentences between subject and predicate. Prepare about six sentences for every pair of students. Store in plastic, zipper bags.

e.g.,

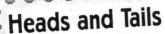

| A strong wind | blew the leaves off the trees. |
| The big red train | disappeared into the tunnel. |

Give each pair of students a bag and ask them to join the heads and tails. Heads begin with a capital letter and tails end in a period.

When assembled, they should take turns to read to each other. Heads and tails are then placed back in the bag, and passed on to another pair, or stored for reuse.

Variation: Ask the pairs to place an "odd" tail with a head to make a nonsense sentence. Ask them to write one nonsense sentence for sharing.

Sentences

A **sentence** is a group of words, which houses a complete idea. It is "fenced in" by a capital letter and a period. A sentence always makes sense.

We use sentences to talk to each other.

A sentence ALWAYS has a verb.

1. Check the sentences. Be prepared to give a reason for your answer.

a. Sunflowers grow in the field. ☐

b. over the rainbow ☐

c. the driver of the truck ☐

d. Pass the salt. ☐

e. Let's go fly our kites. ☐

f. in the fruit basket ☐

g. Start the motor, please. ☐

h. waiting at the corner ☐

i. I can't play hopscotch. ☐

j. Go away. ☐

2. Find the sentences. Put a box around them.
Place a capital letter and a period in each sentence.

rhys and ella are brother and sister rhys is eight and ella is ten they live on a farm before school, they feed the hens after school, they bring the cows home for milking

3. Write one or two sentences around these ideas.

float

_____

_____

squeal

_____

_____

SENTENCES

Sentences - Statements

Many **sentences** make statements. Each one begins with a capital letter and ends in a period. (Examples: I live in America. They are playing marbles. Cows give us milk to drink.)

1. Write a statement about each picture.

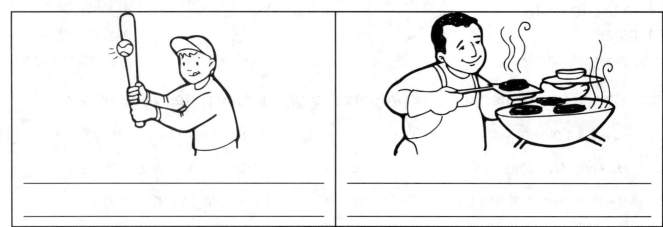

_____

_____

Statements are facts OR opinions.

A **fact** is true.
An **opinion** is what someone thinks is true.

2. Are these statements facts or opinions?

a. Earth is a planet.   _____

b. Everyone needs a cell phone.   _____

c. Apples have a few seeds.   _____

d. The eagle is America's favorite bird.   _____

e. Eating carrots makes your teeth strong.   _____

3. Write one FACT and one OPINION about your school.

_____

_____

_____

SENTENCES

Sentences - Questions

Many sentences ask questions and expect answers. Each one begins with a capital letter and ends in a question mark. (Examples: What is your name? Did you make a cake? Why did you call me? Can you sing?)

1. Here are some quick questions.
   Write your answers as statements.

   a. How many legs does a table have?

   _____

   b. What are two things you would find in a book?

   _____

   c. Where would you buy a parrot?

   _____

   d. How long is a ruler?

   _____

2. Ask someone questions of your own. Don't forget a question mark. Ask a friend to write the answers. Here are some question starters.

   a. Have you seen _____

   _____

   b. What do you _____

   _____

   c. Can you _____

   _____

SENTENCES

Sentences - Exclamations

Some sentences show sudden surprise, anger, or excitement. They are called **exclamations**. Each one begins with a capital letter and ends in an exclamation mark. (Examples: Stop! Help me! Get out of my way! Look over there!)

1. Complete each sentence with a period or an exclamation mark.

a. We have dinner at seven o'clock

b. Everybody stand back

c. What a wonderful surprise

d. Let's go swimming in the pool

e. Look behind you

2. Write an exclamation for each picture.

3. Draw a picture to match these exclamations.

Thank you!
This is just what I wanted!

Hurry! The house is on fire!

SENTENCES

Sentences - Commands

Many sentences give commands and expect action. Each one begins with a capital letter and ends in a period. (Examples: Open the window gently. Add an egg to the mixture. Leave it on the table.)

> **Commands** begin with a <u>verb</u> in the present tense.

1. **Underline the verb in each command.**
   What do you notice? _____

   a. Throw the ball to me, Jess.

   b. Make your bed, please.

   c. Carry the groceries into the kitchen.

   d. Hang the wash on the clothesline.

   e. Turn right at the next corner.

2. **Write your own commands. Begin with these verbs.**

   a. Wash _____

   b. Close _____

   c. Write _____

   d. Go and get _____

   e. Put _____

3. **Write a statement <u>and</u> a command using the word *look*.**

   _____

   _____

SENTENCES

Simple Sentences 1

A **simple sentence** has two main parts:
– the <u>subject</u>: who or what the sentence is about
– the <u>predicate</u>: the verb and the rest of the sentence.

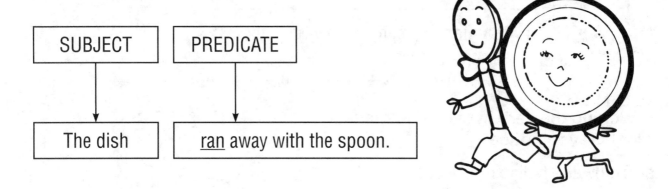

SUBJECT	PREDICATE
The dish	<u>ran</u> away with the spoon.

1. **Underline the "doing" verb. Box the subject. To find the subject, ask who or what is doing the action.**

    a. A honeybee flew back to its hive.

    b. The little kitten sleeps in the old armchair.

    c. The school bus stopped to pick us up.

    d. My uncle lives on a farm in Texas.

    e. The fat, brown spider spun a sticky web.

2. **Complete by adding the rest of each sentence (predicate).**

    a. The mountain climber _____

    b. A green tree snake _____

    c. Mr. Jiggs, the barber, _____

    d. Only five passengers _____

    e. The lost kitten _____

    f. Nina's pet parrot _____

Simple Sentences 2

A **simple sentence** has a subject and a predicate, which contains the verb.

1. Show the simple sentences by coloring the subject and its predicate. Use a different color for each sentence.

a. The wheat in the field	may see a rainbow after the rain.
b. Wind	cooked meat on the barbeque.
c. The freight train	filled the sails of the ship.
d. Dad and Uncle Bill	fell silently all night.
e. You	sped along the railway lines.
f. Soft, white snowflakes	is ripe and golden.

2. Write the subject for each sentence. Use the words in the box below to help you.

our team	Your backpack	The children
The rancher	the spider	Sunflowers

a. _____ has closed the corral gate.

b. At the football game, _____ lost one goal.

c. _____ grow in the garden.

d. _____ sang songs from India.

e. Silently at night, _____ spun its web.

f. _____ is hanging on the doorknob.

SENTENCES

Sentences - Adjectives and Adverbs

Sentences are made more descriptive and interesting by adding adjectives. Adjectives add meaning to nouns. (Example: The <u>strong</u> elephant lifted the <u>heavy</u> logs.)

1. **Add adjectives to describe the nouns.**

    a. The _____ car crashed into a tree.

    b. A soldier stepped from his _____ jeep.

    c. The _____ boys ate all the _____ sandwiches.

    d. There is a _____ box on the _____ table.

    e. A _____ truck roared down the _____ street.

    f. The _____ helicopter landed in the _____ airstrip.

> **Sentences** are made more descriptive and interesting by adding adverbs. Adverbs add meaning to verbs. Look at the examples below.
> The mountain climber fell <u>heavily</u>. (how)
> <u>Last week</u>, the mountain climber fell. (when)
> The mountain climber fell <u>down a cliff</u>. (where)

2. **Add adverbs to add meaning to the verbs.**

    a. The boy walked _____ to the door. (<u>how</u>)

    b. Storm clouds gathered _____. (<u>where</u>)

    c. _____, we went to the rain forest. (<u>when</u>)

    d. The rocket landed _____. (<u>where</u>)

    e. The car raced _____ around the track. (<u>how</u>)

    f. _____ a storm lashed the city. (<u>when</u>)

Compound Sentences

Two simple sentences, joined together, make a **compound sentence**.
(Examples: I like apples, <u>and</u> Jane likes plums.
I wanted to go, <u>but</u> I didn't have a ticket.

1. Join the two sentences, using these joining words:

and	but	so

Some joining words are: <u>and</u>, <u>but</u>, and <u>so</u>.

a. We got on the bus, _____ we went to school.

b. Emma likes pancakes, _____ Madison likes eggs.

c. I am hungry, _____ I will eat lunch.

d. She called his name, _____ he didn't hear her.

e. He wanted a model plane, _____ he saved his money.

f. Pia likes jelly beans, _____ she likes chocolate candies.

2. Join the two sentences with a conjunction (*and*, *so*, *but*).

a. Tom wants to go in the pool, _____ he can't swim.

b. Mia has black hair, _____ Jacqui is blonde.

c. The bell has rung, _____ you may go home.

d. Greg knocked on the door, _____ no one answered.

e. I like coffee, _____ I also like tea.

f. It rained heavily, _____ the water tank is full.

SENTENCES

Sentences in Dialogue

People talk to each other in words and sentences. When we write down what they say, we need quotation marks around those words. We also need to say who is speaking.

"Hello, Millie. Where are you going?" Jayne asked.
"I'm going to visit my Aunty Jean," replied Millie.
"She lives on Piper Street."
"That's near my street," said Jayne.
"Would you like to walk with me?"

1. **Underline the words the people are saying. Then write who said them.**

   a. "I can't find my other sock," groaned Katy. _____

   b. "Did you look under your bed?" asked Mom. _____

   c. "Have you looked in the sock drawer?" asked Sue. _____

   d. "It's probably in the hamper," said Dad. _____

   e. "Oh, here it is," said Katy. "It was in my other shoe." _____

2. **Underline the words the people are saying. Then put quotation marks around them.**

   a. Would you like me to read another story? asked the teacher.

   b. Tilly smiled and said, Thank you for being so kind.

   c. The truck driver shouted, Get out of my way!

   d. Do you have a new bike, William? asked Mr. Pitt.

   e. It's raining, said Sam. Let's go inside.

NOTE: Spoken words are separated from the other words by a comma, a question mark, or an exclamation mark.

SENTENCES

Assessment - Sentences

CHECK 1: Check only the sentences. Give them capital letters and periods. ☐ /5

   a. wheat is growing in the field ☐   **f.** in the piggy bank ☐

   b. over the rolling sea ☐   **g.** cut two pieces of string ☐

   c. the driver of the bus ☐   **h.** standing on tiptoes ☐

   d. wait for me ☐   **i.** she doesn't like olives ☐

   e. let's have some ice cream ☐   **j.** feeling sorry for himself ☐

CHECK 2: Circle the subjects of these sentences. ☐ /5

   a. The men slowly crossed the hot desert on their camels.

   b. After five minutes, the soup was ready to eat.

   c. In the winter, Jasmine will fly to France.

   d. The crowd stood and cheered when the United States won.

   e. Only five people were waiting for the bus.

CHECK 3: Unscramble the questions and punctuate. ☐ /3

   a. for today you What eat did lunch

_____

   b. planes do How make you paper

_____

   c. wearing a you backpack are Why

_____

CHECK 4: Write a question about each subject. ☐ /2

(a lost puppy) _____

(a red bike) _____

          #2433 Targeting Grammar

SENTENCES

CHECK 5: Circle the verbs in these commands. □ /3

    a. Wash your face and hands, please.

    b. Cut the pizza into eight pieces.

    c. Feed your dog once a day.

CHECK 6: Unscramble these commands and punctuate. □ /2

    a. sandwiches our some for slice cheese

    _____

    b. socks on and shoes your put

    _____

CHECK 7: Put in the correct joining words—*and*, *but*, or *so*. □ /3

    a. I have black hair, _____ Joel has black hair as well.

    b. She wanted to go, _____ she was too young.

    c. Ben was tired, _____ he went to bed.

CHECK 8: Join the sentences to make compound sentences. □ /2

    a. Joy bought a brush. She also bought a comb.

    _____

    b. I wanted to read my book. I left it at home.

    _____

CHECK 9: Punctuate this short dialogue. □ /2

    Where will I pin up my picture Bobby asked the teacher

    The teacher replied Please put it on the wall near the door

SENTENCES

CHECK 10: Write a statement and a question about each subject. ☐ /4

a soccer ball _____

_____

a violin _____

_____

CHECK 11: Write an exclamation for each picture. ☐ /3

CHECK 12: Capitalize and punctuate the following text. ☐ /6

An emu is an Australian bird it has wings

but it cannot fly have you ever seen one

SENTENCES

Student Name: _____

Date: _____   Total Score: _____/40

TARGETING GRAMMAR

GAMES & ACTIVITIES

Wordworks

This set of materials is designed for use by students, working
independently or in pairs, to improve their knowledge
(and language) of grammar.

Teachers (and helpers) train, monitor,
scaffold, and intervene as needed.
During each session, students are
encouraged to use their dictionaries.

A *Wordworks* record of achievement
matrix can be maintained as a
personal record of cards completed by
students.

The emphasis is always on learning
and reflecting on that learning, not on
the number of cards completed by any
one student.

Students will become familiar with the terms:

- Verbal adjectives
- Antonyms
- Compound words
- Nouns
- Noun phrases
- Adjectives
- Pronouns
- Gender nouns
- Adverbs
- Gender
- Plurals
- Contractions
- Verbs—doing
- Verbs—saying
- Tense
- Subjects

Preparing the Materials

1. Copy the task cards onto cardstock and laminate for durability.
2. Cut out the cards and store in a small box. (A gift box is ideal.)
3. Copy, cut, and store the information on this page with the materials.
4. Copy the progress chart—sufficient for one per student. Ask them to glue it into a specified workbook.
5. As a card is completed and corrected, the student colors the corresponding number on the progress chart.

PROGRESS CHART   *Wordworks*   Name:

1	2	3	4	5	6	7	8	9	10	11	12	13	14	15

16	17	18	19	20	21	22	23	24	25	26	27	28	29	30

PROGRESS CHART   *Wordworks*   Name:

1	2	3	4	5	6	7	8	9	10	11	12	13	14	15

16	17	18	19	20	21	22	23	24	25	26	27	28	29	30

PROGRESS CHART   *Wordworks*   Name:

1	2	3	4	5	6	7	8	9	10	11	12	13	14	15

16	17	18	19	20	21	22	23	24	25	26	27	28	29	30

PROGRESS CHART   *Wordworks*   Name:

1	2	3	4	5	6	7	8	9	10	11	12	13	14	15

16	17	18	19	20	21	22	23	24	25	26	27	28	29	30

1 VERBAL ADJECTIVES
Finding matching nouns.

★ cooking	★ peanuts
★ swimming	★ truck
★ running	★ person
★ caring	★ pool
★ crowded	★ beans
★ loaded	★ pot
★ baked	★ street
★ roasted	★ shoes

Wordworks

2 ANTONYMS
Match words of opposite meaning.

★ lost	★ rough
★ fresh	★ west
★ smooth	★ found
★ late	★ early
★ sharp	★ young
★ old	★ low
★ high	★ stale
★ east	★ dull

Wordworks

3 SEE, SAW, OR SEEN?
Complete each sentence correctly.

★ Have you ever _____ snow?

★ Did you _____ John come in?

★ We _____ lots of red balloons.

★ The men didn't want to be _____.

★ Tim was sure he had _____ a mouse.

★ I didn't _____ what you _____.

Wordworks

4 COMPOUND WORDS
Join two words to make a new one.

★ coast	★ way
★ home	★ flakes
★ head	★ line
★ fire	★ lights
★ drive	★ wood
★ pop	★ work
★ bed	★ room
★ corn	★ corn

Wordworks

5 ADJECTIVES and NOUNS
Find the words that go together.

★ slithering	★ lemon
★ crunchy	★ pencil
★ funny	★ person
★ sharp	★ log
★ dangerous	★ snake
★ heavy	★ clown
★ elderly	★ apple
★ sour	★ fire

Wordworks

6 NOUNS and ADJECTIVES
Sort into two columns.

★ happy	★ candle
★ kitchen	★ large
★ boat	★ computer
★ busy	★ lazy
★ football	★ sweet
★ crunchy	★ people
★ long	★ simple
★ clock	★ kangaroo

Wordworks

NOUNS and VERBS
Sort the nouns
and verbs.

★ riddle   ★ juggle
★ kettle   ★ jungle
★ stumble   ★ struggle
★ sizzle   ★ table
★ title   ★ dazzle

Wordworks

 CONTRACTIONS
What words have
been replaced?

★ they're   ★ can't
★ we've   ★ won't
★ I've   ★ couldn't
★ they'd   ★ don't
★ it's   ★ hasn't

Wordworks

 ADJECTIVES
Write two adjectives to
describe each noun.

★ book   ★ car
★ plate   ★ weather
★ coat   ★ tree
★ hat   ★ balloon
★ crow   ★ house

Wordworks

 **ADJECTIVES
to ADVERBS**
Change the adjectives to adverbs, using "–ly."
Note the rules for "y," and "final e."

★ happy   ★ hungry
★ easy   ★ safe
★ glad   ★ lazy
★ gentle   ★ usual
★ quick   ★ most
★ noisy   ★ bright

Wordworks

 PAST TENSE VERBS
Write the past tense form
of each verb.

★ do   ★ hop
★ are   ★ ring
★ has   ★ is
★ find   ★ fall
★ grow   ★ sit
★ cry   ★ see

Wordworks

 ADDING –*ING*
Note the doubling rule
and the "final e" rule.

★ run   ★ tumble
★ like   ★ crash
★ dry   ★ bend
★ snow   ★ cut
★ sit   ★ decide
★ leave   ★ wash

Wordworks

13. NOUNS and ADJECTIVES

Sort into the correct columns.

★ pie
★ warm
★ enormous
★ tale
★ garden
★ sunny
★ angel
★ interesting

★ helpful
★ spaceship
★ pickle
★ careless
★ prince
★ violin
★ friendly
★ tasty

Wordworks

14. SUGGEST A SUITABLE NOUN

★ a long, straight _____
★ hot, salty _____
★ an interesting _____
★ a round, red _____
★ an old, tattered _____
★ a tall, dark-haired _____
★ a clean, new _____
★ a yellow, plastic _____
★ a sudden, loud _____

Wordworks

15. SUBJECT and PREDICATE

Complete by adding a predicate.

★ A black spider _____
★ The girl with red hair _____
★ The football player _____
★ For my birthday, I _____
★ Some children _____
★ The yellow moon _____

Wordworks

16. DID or DONE?

Complete each sentence correctly.

★ James _____ his homework.
★ Have you _____ yours?
★ No, I have not _____ mine yet.
★ Tom _____ his at five o'clock.
★ Jill had hers _____ before dinner.
★ Molly _____ not do hers at all.

Wordworks

17. COMPOUND WORDS

Join a word from each list.

★ post
★ tooth
★ goal
★ hand
★ broom
★ foot
★ rain
★ eye

★ drops
★ ball
★ card
★ lashes
★ keeper
★ pick
★ stick
★ bag

Wordworks

18. PLURALS

Write the plural form
of the following.

★ grape _____
★ pencil _____
★ baby _____
★ child _____
★ banana _____
★ leaf _____
★ woman _____
★ passenger _____

Wordworks

19 HOW, WHEN, or WHERE?
Complete by saying more
about the verb.

★ Put your shoes **under** _____.
★ **Last** _____, we flew to Japan.
★ **During** _____, we swim every day.
★ The horse walked **towards** _____.
★ We all wore crazy hats **to** _____.
★ Dad reads the paper **every** _____.
★ The frightened bird flew **out** _____.
★ The clever dog jumped **through** _____.

20 SUBJECT SEARCH
Find the subject of each sentence.

★ Ducks and geese live on our farm.
★ Her yellow, straw hat blew away.
★ Fierce tigers live in the jungle.
★ Writing stories is fun.
★ A long road led to the town.
★ Last week, Bob and I went camping.
★ Mary is ready to sing her song.
★ Everyone in the class likes pizza.

21 WORD SORTS
Sort the words into three categories:
MALE, FEMALE, or EITHER

★ cow   ★ rooster

★ teacher   ★ husband

★ nephew   ★ queen

★ athlete   ★ uncle

★ niece   ★ pilot

★ adult   ★ aunt

22 CONTRACTIONS
What words do these
take the place of?

★ you've   ★ didn't
★ I'll   ★ hadn't
★ she's   ★ wouldn't
★ they're   ★ doesn't
★ we're   ★ aren't
★ you're   ★ weren't
★ I'm   ★ can't
★ he'd   ★ wasn't

23 VERBS
Sort the verbs into
SAYING or DOING.

★ sprint   ★ chat

★ stammer   ★ grumble

★ travel   ★ sail

★ boil   ★ boast

★ say   ★ build

24 STATEMENTS and QUESTIONS
Write one statement and one question
using these words.

★ right

★ plane

★ rabbit

★ rain

★ tunnel

25 NOUN SORTS
Sort into four categories:
ANIMAL PERSON PLACE THING

- ★ monkey
- ★ supermarket
- ★ dentist
- ★ spade
- ★ gymnast
- ★ koala
- ★ fence
- ★ park
- ★ pilot
- ★ India
- ★ zebra
- ★ ladder
- ★ gardener
- ★ torch
- ★ deer
- ★ kitchen

Wordworks

26 ANTONYMS
Match words
of opposite meaning.

- ★ tame
- ★ honest
- ★ fast
- ★ straight
- ★ long
- ★ wide
- ★ crooked
- ★ short
- ★ wild
- ★ narrow
- ★ slow
- ★ dishonest

Wordworks

27 WENT or GONE?
Complete each
sentence correctly.

- ★ Everyone has _____ home.
- ★ We _____ to visit Aunt Jenny.
- ★ The actors _____ on stage.
- ★ He has _____ to the library.
- ★ The food on the table has _____.
- ★ Our class _____ to the rain forest.
- ★ The sign said, "_____ Fishing."

Wordworks

28 HELPING VERBS
Add a helper to the verb.

- ★ I _____ going to the dentist.
- ★ He _____ eaten his dinner.
- ★ They _____ come tomorrow.
- ★ He _____ waiting for the bus.
- ★ She _____ swim very well.
- ★ We _____ playing soccer.

Wordworks

29 ADJECTIVE SORTS
Sort into three categories
to describe:
PERSON, PLACE, or THING

- ★ plastic
- ★ crowded
- ★ grassy
- ★ clever
- ★ strong
- ★ striped
- ★ sandy
- ★ friendly
- ★ broken
- ★ tasty
- ★ helpful
- ★ rocky

Wordworks

30 CONTRACTIONS
Contract these subjects
and verbs.

- ★ She will
- ★ I have
- ★ He is
- ★ You are
- ★ We have
- ★ I would
- ★ They are
- ★ She would
- ★ I am
- ★ It is
- ★ You have
- ★ We are

Wordworks

Grammar Flaps

Preparation of Materials

1. Copy all the Grammar Flaps onto cardstock. Cut out all the cards. Laminate for durability.

2. Cut along the dashed line of each card. Attach this bottom strip to the line on the Grammar Flaps card to make a flap that covers the answers.

3. Do this by placing a piece of double-sided tape on the underside of the flap.

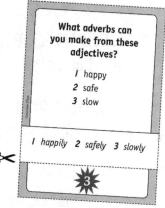

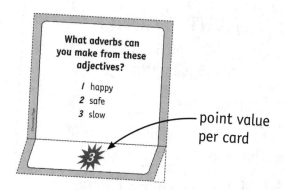

point value per card

How to Play

1. Two players challenge each other to a game.

2. Shuffle the cards and place facedown between the two players. Place a box of counters on the table also.

3. Player 1 draws the top card and asks Player 2 the question or direction. For example: "For four points, what is the past tense of these verbs?" For each correct answer, Player 1 gives Player 2 a counter. Player 1 checks the answers by lifting the flap.

4. Some cards are marked with "(Spelling Bonus)." This means that a player can win an additional point for each answer correctly spelled.

5. Player 2 now has a turn asking the question.

6. When all cards have been played, the players count all the counters they have won. The player with the most counters wins.

NOTE: This game may be played by a small group. In this case, a player would ask the person on his or her left for an answer.

What are the plurals of these nouns?

1. peach
2. child
3. tooth
4. mouse

(Spelling Bonus)

---

1. peaches   3. teeth
2. children   4. mice

What are antonyms (opposites) of these adjectives?

1. wild
2. smooth
3. fresh

---

1. tame   2. rough   3. stale

What are the contractions of these words?

1. will not
2. cannot
3. was not

---

1. won't   2. can't   3. wasn't

Name two compound nouns beginning with:

foot

---

footprint   footpath
football   footwork

What is the past tense of these verbs?

1. play
2. bring
3. blow
4. see

---

1. played
2. brought
3. blew
4. saw

What adverbs can you make from these adjectives?

1. happy
2. safe
3. slow

---

1. happily　　2. safely　　3. slowly

Which adjective does NOT describe the noun:

orange: juicy, round, tall

slipper: soft, plastic, warm

teeth: lazy, clean, white

---

1. tall　　2. plastic　　3. lazy

Which word in each group is NOT a noun?

1. ribbon, fast, pie
2. house, floor, straight
3. pretty, dollar, farm

---

1. fast　　2. straight　　3. pretty

What is the missing pronoun?

1. She waited for _____ friend.
2. They gave _____ mother roses.
3. Keep _____ hands to yourself.
4. I took _____ bat to school.

(Spelling Bonus)

1. her   3. your
2. their   4. my

What is the correct spelling —*their* or *there*?

1. Put your hats over _____.
2. They had _____ dinner early.
3. _____ dad has a motorbike.
4. I knew she'd be _____.

1. there   3. Their
2. their   4. there

What is the correct word—*who* or *what*?

1. _____ likes jelly beans?
2. _____ is on the phone?
3. _____ are you doing?
4. _____ was late today?
5. _____ is in the box?

1. Who   3. What   5. What
2. Who   4. Who

What are the plurals of these nouns?

1. leaf
2. lady
3. knife
4. dish

(Spelling Bonus)

1. leaves   3. knives
2. ladies   4. dishes

What two words have been contracted?

1. she's
2. we're
3. you've
4. it's

---

1. she is/has   3. you have
2. we are   4. it is

Name two compounds nouns beginning with:

door

---

doorstop   doorstep   doorbell
doorknob   doorway   doorman

Which is the correct word —*which* or *what*?

1. Choose _____ book you want.
2. I didn't know _____ to think.
3. _____ way did he go?
4. _____ did you see?
5. You can buy _____ you want.

---

1. which   3. Which   5. what
2. what   4. What

Name the correct word —*saw* or *seen*.

1. Have you _____ a zebra?
2. I _____ a street parade.
3. They _____ the game.
4. We have not _____ him.
5. He had never _____ snow.

---

1. seen   3. saw   5. seen
2. saw   4. seen

Name the tense (time).

(past, present, future)

1. We will play dominoes.
2. I threw the ball high.
3. He is reading a book.
4. Tom was eating a pie.
5. Shall we go tomorrow?

1. future   3. present   5. future
2. past   4. past

Can you correct these sentences?

1. He went <u>down</u> the ladder to the roof.
2. We will go fly kites <u>yesterday</u>.
3. Jack ran <u>slowly</u> and won the race.

1. up   2. tomorrow   3. fast or quickly

What are the subjects?

1. A bee flew to the flower.
2. My uncle lives on a farm.
3. On Sunday, I will go home.
4. My friend is here.
5. Six people got on the bus.

1. A bee   3. I   5. Six people
2. My uncle   4. My friend

What is the male form of these words?

1. queen
2. aunt
3. ladies
4. hen

1. king   3. gentlemen
2. uncle   4. rooster

GRAND SLAM

Preparation of Materials

Copy, laminate, and cut out the Grand Slam cards. There are six games requiring players to use cloze sentences with nouns, adjectives, pronouns, verbs, adverbs, or contractions. There are eighteen cards per game. Each completed sentence has a point value.

Secure each game with a rubber band, or store in a plastic, zipper bag.

How to Play

1. Select a **Grand Slam** game. Place all cards facedown in rows on the table.

2. Players take turns. A player selects two cards and reads what is on them—either a sentence or a word. If they "match," the player takes the pair and has another turn. If not, the player returns the two cards to their original positions. The next player has a turn.

3. If a player picks up a **Grand Slam** card, he or she keeps it to count toward his or her final score. The player selects another card in its place.

4. Play continues until all cards have been won.

Scoring

Players count the points on the cards they have won, plus any **Grand Slam** points. The one with the highest number of points wins.

GRAND SLAM I

Some birds look for worms and _____ in the ground.

People often add salt and _____ to their food.

GRAND SLAM

③

_____ is a very fast game played on ice.

There are five _____ on a basketball team.

In football, a player kicks the ball over the _____.

The mother kangaroo carries her baby in her _____.

The _____ is a relative of the dog.

We bought apples, bananas, plums, and grapes at the _____.

GRAND SLAM I

Nouns

I pouch 1 GRAND SLAM	I Hockey 2 GRAND SLAM	I insects 1 GRAND SLAM
I wolf 1 GRAND SLAM	I players 2 GRAND SLAM	I pepper 1 GRAND SLAM
I supermarket 2 GRAND SLAM	I goalpost 2 GRAND SLAM	I GRAND SLAM 3 GRAND SLAM

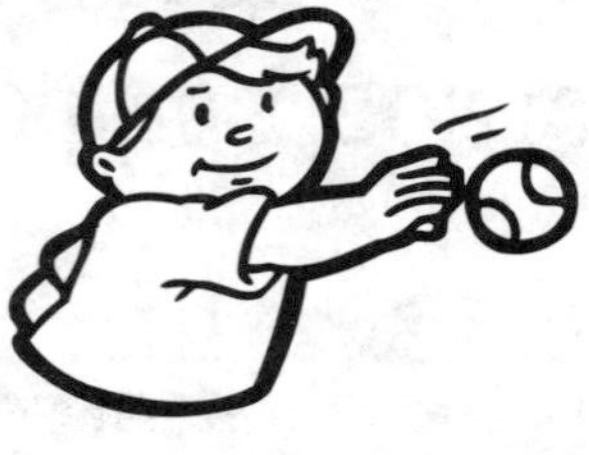

GRAND SLAM 2

I bought a loaf of _____ bread at the bakery.

GRAND SLAM

②

She walked on the beach in her _____ hat and sandals.

GRAND SLAM

②

---

③

GRAND SLAM

GRAND SLAM

②

Chris is the _____ runner in our class.

GRAND SLAM

②

After a long day in the fields, the farmer was very _____ .

GRAND SLAM

②

He has _____ cheese sandwiches in his lunch box.

GRAND SLAM

②

A parrot has very _____ feathers.

GRAND SLAM

②

The _____ boy rushed out and slammed the door.

GRAND SLAM

②

The teacher told us some _____ facts about crocodiles.

GRAND SLAM

②

GRAND SLAM 2

Adjectives

colorful **2**	fastest **1**	wheat **2**
angry **1**	tired **1**	straw **1**
interesting **2**	tasty **2**	**GRAND SLAM** **3**

GRAND SLAM

GRAND SLAM 3

3 · I put my name on the book because it was _____.

GRAND SLAM

3 · I would like you to come to _____ birthday party on Saturday.

GRAND SLAM

3 · **GRAND SLAM**

GRAND SLAM

③

3 · Did you hand _____ ticket to the man at the gate?

GRAND SLAM

3 · Maria put on _____ green shorts and a red T-shirt.

GRAND SLAM

3 · Jack took _____ pet bird to school to show his class.

GRAND SLAM

3 · They took _____ books back to the library.

GRAND SLAM

3 · Tilly is arriving soon. _____ is my aunt.

GRAND SLAM

3 · We told _____ to wait, but they wouldn't listen.

GRAND SLAM

GRAND SLAM 3

Pronouns

mine ①	your ②	their ①
my ①	her ②	She ①
GRAND SLAM ③	his ②	them ②

GRAND SLAM 4

GRAND SLAM ③

The farmer ____ wheat in the field.

GRAND SLAM

The twins ____ together on the trampoline.

GRAND SLAM

One player ____ three touchdowns in the football game.

GRAND SLAM

We watched as the plane ____ on the runway.

GRAND SLAM

The two friends ____ on the phone for an hour.

GRAND SLAM

Miss Prim will ____ how to make pancakes.

GRAND SLAM

Which computer game did you ____ ?

GRAND SLAM

Did you ____ cereal and toast for breakfast?

GRAND SLAM

GRAND SLAM 4

Verbs

planted ①	jump ②	scored ①
landed ①	talked ②	explain ①
buy ②	have ②	GRAND SLAM ③

GRAND SLAM 5

③

GRAND SLAM

GRAND SLAM

---

5 | Rain fell _____ all through the night.

GRAND SLAM

5 | Come and sit _____ with me.

GRAND SLAM

---

5 | You go now. I'll come _____.

GRAND SLAM

5 | The sun is going _____ in the west, and the moon is rising in the east.

GRAND SLAM

5 | If we go to the game _____, we will get _____ good seats.

GRAND SLAM

---

5 | A crab walks _____.

GRAND SLAM

5 | I like to play _____, but on wet days I have to stay inside.

GRAND SLAM

5 | How _____ do you go to the beach?

GRAND SLAM

GRAND SLAM 5

Adverbs

heavily — 1

here — 1

GRAND SLAM — 3

later — 2

down — 2

early — 2

sideways — 1

outside — 1

often — 2

Contractions

⑥ Mom told Jason he <u>couldn't</u> go to the skateboard park today.

GRAND SLAM

⑥ I <u>don't</u> know how to fold a paper airplane.

GRAND SLAM

⑥ Tom <u>wasn't</u> sure how to answer my question.

GRAND SLAM

⑥ The teacher called us on stage, but we <u>weren't</u> ready.

GRAND SLAM

⑥ <u>It's</u> such fun going to see all the animals at the zoo.

GRAND SLAM

⑥ <u>Who's</u> been using my scissors and glue?

GRAND SLAM

⑥ <u>They're</u> not here yet, so I guess <u>they're</u> not coming.

GRAND SLAM

⑥ <u>You've</u> been told not to climb on the fence!

GRAND SLAM

⑥ **GRAND SLAM**

GRAND SLAM

③

GRAND SLAM 6

① **was not**

GRAND SLAM

⑥

② **do not**

GRAND SLAM

⑥

① **could not**

GRAND SLAM

⑥

① **Who has**

GRAND SLAM

⑥

② **It is**

GRAND SLAM

⑥

① **were not**

GRAND SLAM

⑥

③ **GRAND SLAM**

GRAND SLAM

⑥

② **You have**

GRAND SLAM

⑥

② **They are**

GRAND SLAM

⑥

A word game for two to four players

Preparation

Copy the Tactics! baseboards (one per player), the word cards, and the answer key. Laminate for durability.

How to Play

1. Two to four players challenge each other to a game of Tactics!

2. One other player supervises the game. The supervisor has the answer key to check that the players' answers are correct before they place their cards.

3. Each player has a baseboard. Shuffle the word cards and place them in a stack, facedown on the table.

4. The first player takes the top card off the stack, reads it, and decides where to place it on the baseboard. The supervisor checks the answer and, if correct, the player places it on the correct word category on the baseboard. If incorrect, the card is placed on a "discard" stack, and play goes to the next player.

   If a player has already placed a word card on the board and draws a second word of the same category, he or she places it on top of the first card.

5. The first player to cover all the words on the board is the winner.

6. The winner becomes the supervisor of the next game.

Tactics! Answer Key

Pronouns		Adjectives		Verbs (Present Tense)	
theirs	mine	strong	hungry	wait	sing
its	yours	steep	tasty	likes	is kicking
our	his	hot	soft	write	push

Verbs (Past Tense)		Nouns		Adverbs	
went	jumped	flower	elephant	quietly	yesterday
rang	ate	banana	gate	often	slowly
threw	has done	kitchen	pilot	sometimes	tomorrow

Contractions		Conjunctions			Compound Nouns	
it's	we've				snowflakes	headlights
can't	won't	and	but	so	waterfall	doorway
wasn't	they're				horseback	popcorn

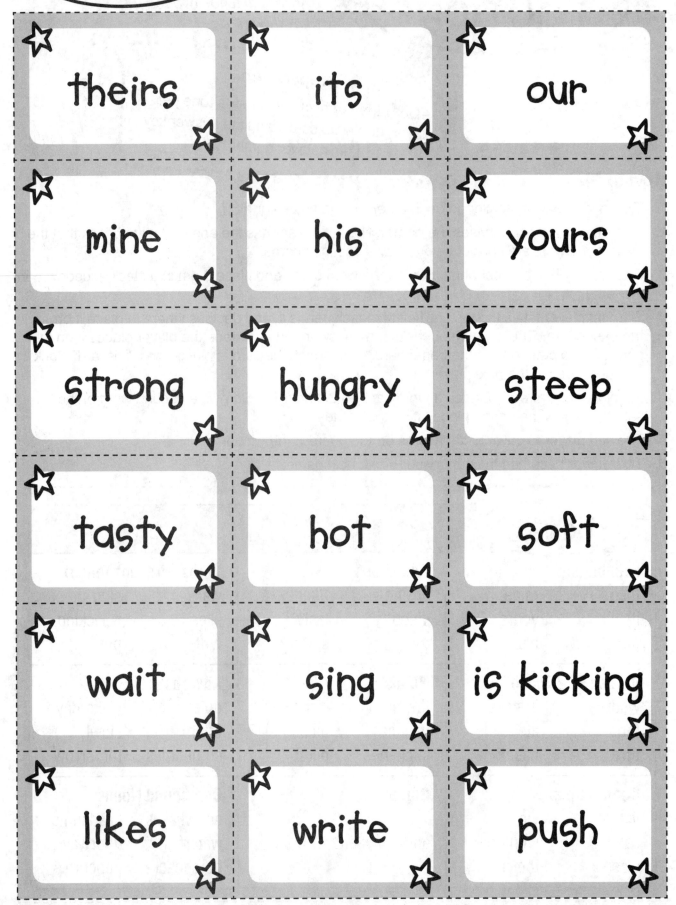

theirs	its	our
mine	his	yours
strong	hungry	steep
tasty	hot	soft
wait	sing	is kicking
likes	write	push

went	jumped	rang
ate	threw	has done
elephant	flower	banana
gate	kitchen	pilot
quietly	often	yesterday
tomorrow	sometimes	slowly

and	but	so
and	but	so
it's	we've	can't
won't	they're	wasn't
snowflakes	headlights	waterfall
popcorn	horseback	doorway

 **Baseboard**

Verb (present tense)	**Adverb**	**Compound Noun**
Adjective	**Noun**	**Conjunction**
Pronoun	**Verb** (past tense)	**Contraction**

GRAMMAR BY NUMBERS 1

*What are the missing **nouns**? Choose the correct noun from the dot-to-dot picture.*

Then place the number of the sentence beside the corresponding dot.

When you have finished all the sentences, join the dots, starting at number 1.

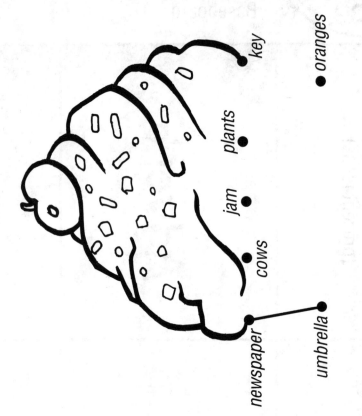

• key

• oranges

• plants

• door

jam •

• finger

cows •

newspaper •

umbrella

• candle

1. The man on the bench is reading

a _____ .

2. The farmer milked the _____
this morning.

3. I like toast and _____ for breakfast.

4. Water the _____ in the garden.

5. I lost the _____ to unlock the door.

6. I bought _____ at the fruit stand.

7. Open the _____ and go in.

8. Jack cut his _____ on a knife.

9. Light your _____ , so we can see.

10. You will need an _____ if it rains.

GRAMMAR BY NUMBERS 2

*What are the missing **adjectives**? Choose the correct adjective from the dot-to-dot picture.*
Then place the number of the sentence beside the corresponding dot.
When you have finished all the sentences, join the dots, starting at number 1.

1. The sky is _____ today.

2. He climbed the old, _____ ladder.

3. Whip the cream until it is _____.

4. I like sweet, _____ peaches.

5. He was _____ when he lost his race.

6. We sat below the _____, green tree.

7. After the rain, the road was _____.

8. My big brother has a _____ bike.

9. The dog was _____, but now he is big.

10. Put your _____ clothes in the wash.

disappointed
leafy
dirty
little
racing
slippery
juicy
Bones
blue
thick
wooden

Grammar by Numbers 3

*What are the missing **pronouns**? Choose the correct pronoun from the dot-to-dot picture.*

Then place the number of the sentence beside the corresponding dot.

When you have finished all the sentences, join the dots, starting at number 1.

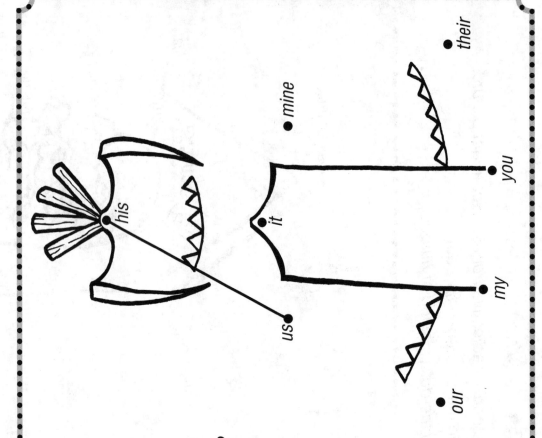

1. My baby brother pulled on _____ socks.

2. Please give the ball back to me. It is _____.

3. They were speaking to _____ friends.

4. Have _____ eaten all your dinner yet?

5. Jeb has a pet bird. He keeps _____ in a cage.

6. I would like you to meet _____ teacher.

7. After we did _____ homework, we watched TV.

8. We are tired. Please wait for _____.

Grammar by Numbers 4

What are the missing **verbs**? Choose the correct verb from the dot-to-dot picture.
Then place the number of the sentence beside the corresponding dot.
When you have finished all the sentences, join the dots, starting at number 1.

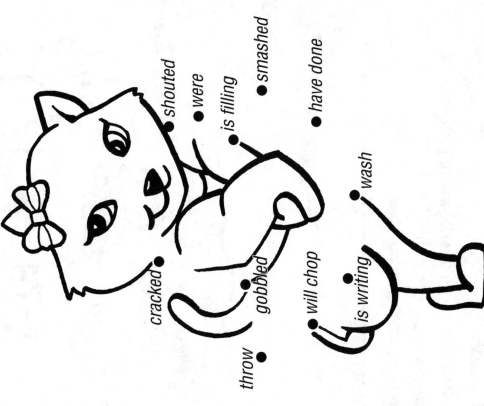

1. The cowboy _____ his whip.

2. The hungry dog _____ up his food.

3. Did you _____ the ball over the fence?

4. Dan _____ the firewood.

5. Liam _____ a letter to his uncle.

6. _____ your hands before dinner.

7. I _____ all my chores.

8. A soccer ball _____ our window.

9. Jane _____ her bucket with water.

10. They _____ hot, dirty, and tired.

11. I _____ loudly, but no one heard me.

GRAMMAR BY NUMBERS 5

*What are the missing **adverbs**? Choose the correct adverb from the dot-to-dot picture.*
Then place the number of the sentence beside the corresponding dot.
When you have finished all the sentences, join the dots, starting at number 1.

sometimes

quickly

slowly

outside

later

east

quietly

loudly

sideways

tightly

when

1. Ben ran _____ to catch the train.

2. He crept _____ past the open window.

3. Let's go _____ and play in the sun.

4. You go to the park. I'll come _____ .

5. The plane flew _____ towards Europe.

6. _____ can we go to the zoo?

7. He tied his shoelaces _____ .

8. They walked _____ like crabs.

9. The bird squawked _____ in the tall tree.

10. Jack sat up in his tree house and read _____ .

11. _____ I go jogging with my dad.

GRAMMAR BY NUMBERS 6

What are the missing contractions? Choose the correct contraction from the dot-to-dot picture.
Then place the number of the sentence beside the corresponding dot.
When you have finished all the sentences, join the dots, starting at number 1.

1. I _____ know how to drive a car yet.

2. Corey _____ see well without his glasses.

3. _____ go swimming tomorrow.

4. _____ the name of the book you are reading?

5. Mom says _____ too late to go for a walk.

6. Kenji _____ very happy yesterday!

7. Sarah _____ come to school today.

8. _____ a hole in my sock!

9. I can't come. I _____ finished my homework.

10. _____ all made their model planes.

11. _____ only a little girl.

12. _____ knocking on the door?

Dots: they've • haven't • there's • she's • didn't • wasn't • who's • it's • don't • let's • can't • what's

GRAMMAR BY NUMBERS 7

What are the missing antonyms? Choose the correct antonym from the dot-to-dot picture.

Then place the number of the sentence beside the corresponding dot.

When you have finished all the sentences, join the dots, starting at number 1.

1. I went up the hill as he came _____ .

2. A tortoise is _____ , but a rabbit is fast.

3. He was sad for awhile, but now he is _____ .

4. The river is _____ , but the creek is narrow.

5. I will replace your _____ hat with a new one.

6. Ben is short, but his brother is very _____ .

7. Cut the long piece of string into _____ pieces.

8. My face was clean, but now it is _____ .

9. The cakes are _____ , but the bread is stale.

10. An apple is smooth, but a coconut is _____ .

11. The old lady gave the _____ boy an apple.

12. Joe went under the fence, but I went _____ it.

13. The bus arrives at six and _____ at seven.

happy

wide

old

tall

short

dirty

fresh

rough

slow

down

leaves

over

young

GRAMMAR BY NUMBERS 8

*What are the missing **compound words**? Choose the correct compound words from the dot-to-dot picture.*

Then place the number of the sentence beside the corresponding dot.

When you have finished all the sentences, join the dots, starting at number 1.

1. Did you hear the _____ crack his whip?

2. The driver switched on the _____ of his car.

3. The _____ pumps water into the tank.

4. There's a _____ in the cornfield.

5. The _____ blocked the ball.

6. I brush my teeth in the _____.

7. A shoe box is made of _____.

8. The sky is filled with bright colors at _____.

9. The boys are playing _____.

10. We walked down the _____ towards home.

11. The plane landed safely on the _____.

12. Mom carries her money in her _____.

goalkeeper

•scarecrow

•windmill

bathroom•

•headlights

•cowboy

handbag

cardboard•

•baseball

runway

sunset•

footpath

GRAMMAR BY NUMBERS 9

*What are the missing **question words**? Choose the correct words from the dot-to-dot picture.*

Then place the number of the sentence beside the corresponding dot.

When you have finished all the sentences, join the dots, starting at number 1.

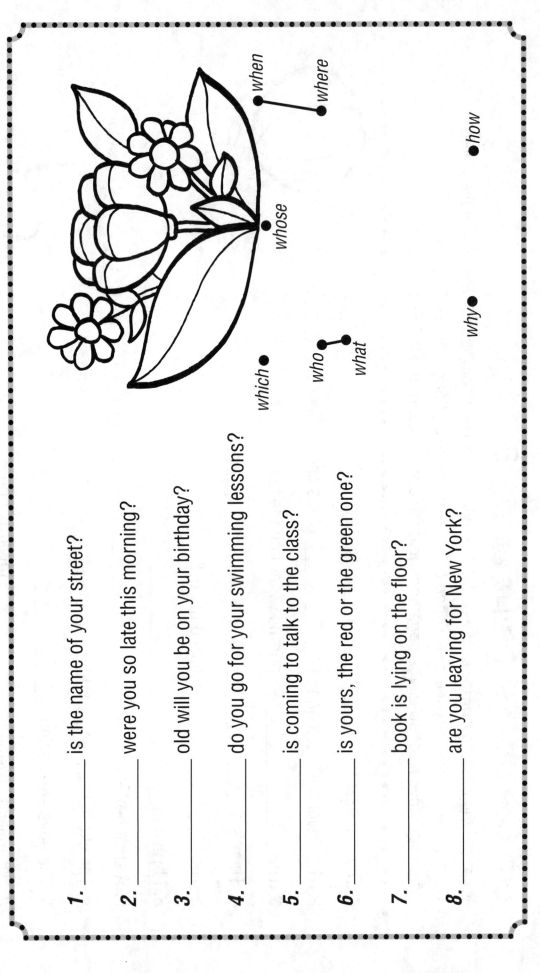

1. _____ is the name of your street?

2. _____ were you so late this morning?

3. _____ old will you be on your birthday?

4. _____ do you go for your swimming lessons?

5. _____ is coming to talk to the class?

6. _____ is yours, the red or the green one?

7. _____ book is lying on the floor?

8. _____ are you leaving for New York?

GRAMMAR BY NUMBERS 10

*What are the missing **verbs**? Choose the correct verb from the dot-to-dot picture.*
Then place the number of the sentence beside the corresponding dot.
When you have finished all the sentences, join the dots, starting at number 1.

1. _____ your hands with soap and water.

2. _____ a song for me.

3. _____ how many chairs we need, please.

4. _____ out the window and tell me what you see.

5. _____ me a picture with your watercolors.

6. _____ off the light and go to sleep.

7. _____ two tablespoons of sugar.

8. _____ your book to the person beside you.

9. _____ off the water faucet.

10. _____ the bean seeds in your garden.

11. _____ this broom and sweep the floor.

12. _____ a story in your workbook.

13. _____ for everyone to arrive.

14. _____ the door and lock it, please.

Kriss Kross Nouns

Puzzle 1

```
P R Y U S F G B E D
U F K L K B T X E L
M G R W A E E M V G
P T E J T S K R Y A
K Q T H E R S G D T
I C U P B O A R D E
N S P H O H B R Z D
D F M J A L K R S T
N H O U R E F T Y X
D F C H D R E A M Y
```

skateboard   cupboard
hour   gate
basket   computer
dream   bed
pumpkin   horse   **1**

Puzzle 2

```
P R T U S F G P R D
E F R L K E F I N K
F G A W A E C H V G
F T M J T S E S M L
A Q P A L M G H A K
R C O P B O A R M E
I F L O W E R Z M D
G C I B A N A N A T
N H N U R E G T L X
D N E I R F P T M Y
```

flower   friend
trampoline   ship
banana   mammal
palm   knife
garage   giraffe   **2**

Puzzle 3

```
N I F F U M N B E M
U F K L K B E T Z A
M R O T C O D U V C
P T E J T S R R Y H
W Q C H E R A K D I
O B A N D A G E D N
D S R H O C B Y Z E
A F P R I N C E S S
H G E U R E F T Y X
S F T R U M P E T Y
```

machine   shadow
carpet   bandage
muffin   trumpet
doctor   garden
princess   turkey   **3**

Puzzle 4

```
P R T U S E N A L P
U F E L K B T X E L
M G A L F E R M V G
P T C A R R O T Y A
K Q H O U S E G X B
C C E P B H A R D R
A S R H O E B R Z E
R F M J A D K R S A
T I B B A R F T C D
D F N U D H S U R B
```

rabbit   carrot
plane   shed
bread   teacher
flag   track
brush   house   **4**

Kriss Kross   Adjectives

```
S P H I K O H I G H
U O D D K B T S F L
M W R I Y E B F R A
P E A J L S N R I B
K R T H E R S G E L
I F E W V O A R N U
N U G N I C N A D N
D L M J L T K R L T
N H N E Z O R F Y X
R O U N D G I J L Y
```

round   lively
friendly   odd
blunt   high
powerful   dancing
few   frozen   **5**

```
H R Y M F U N N Y D
C F K A K B I X O T
I G R N A E U C N A
R T E Y T W I D E E
K Q T H E R S S D R
S T R O N G K U L G
N S P H O H C N O D
O D A Z Z L I N G T
N H O U R E U Y I N
D F C J D R Q I S Y
```

quick   funny
golden   strong
wide   many
sunny   rich
dazzling   great   **6**

```
E R Y L U F E S U F
L F K L K S L X E A
D G R W A S I M V B
E R T J V E B H H U
R Q E T I L O P A L
L C L A B P M R D O
Y S R L B L B R Z U
D F A L H E A V Y S
N H C U R H F T Y X
L O S A L T Y L E S
```

polite   salty
fabulous   mobile
heavy   helpless
tall   elderly
scarlet   useful   **7**

```
L R H U S F C B Y D
C F S N A U G H T Y
A G E W A E S O W M
R T R J I S O R I A
E J F A M O U S S E
L T I P B I R X T R
E S R H E H B R E C
S F M J D L K R D T
S H I U U E F T Y X
D B E A R D E D M B
```

careless   firm
twisted   naughty
rude   fresh
famous   bearded
creamy   sour   **8**
```
```

Kriss Kross Verbs – present tense

```
E R K B E L I E V E
S H O V E O T X R U
M O R H A S E M V S
P G E H T E K R Y U
K R T H I V S B D B
S O M E R S A U L T
N W O R R O B Y Z R
D F M J A L A R S A
N H O U R E K T R C
D F W R I T E L M T
```

bake	borrow
somersault	write
lose	grow
believe	buy
shove	subtract ⑨

```
O R E U C S E R P D
R F K L K B T I D O
E W R I P E A S I G
M A G R E E K R S A
O I T H E V A E L T
V T U P L R T R I W
E S P H S P E A K A
U F M J A L K R E L
N H O U R E F T Y K
D S C R E A M A I X
```

speak	leave
sleep	remove
walk	agree
rescue	scream
dislike	wait ⑩

```
S R Y U S F G P U T
T F K L K B T X E L
A G O R I D E M V G
Y T E J T S E R Y L
K F T H W A S H D L
I O G P A O A Y D I
N S P H N H B R Z F
D F M J T L K R S T
N H O U R D E E N S
A R E H D R Z A T I
```

stay	fill
need	are
put	ride
go	see
want	wash ⑪

```
D E E L B I O R T D
I O G S D T H N O E
E S M I F E E L V C
P T I J T S K R Y I
K E X P L A I N T D
I A U P B M A R D E
L L P S O H B R Z I
E F G N I R B R S T
A H O X R E F T Y X
K F C H D R T A L K
```

leak	bleed
explain	mix
talk	bring
decide	steal
feel	am ⑫

Kriss Kross

Verbs – past tense

```
A  R  Y  U  S  F  W  K  E  D        P  E  N  B  L  E  W  H  E  D
T  O  L  D  K  B  S  A  I  D        R  F  G  R  K  B  T  Z  J  L
E  G  R  W  A  S  E  M  V  E        M  S  H  O  W  E  D  M  V  D
P  M  E  N  D  E  D  R  Y  B        P  T  E  U  T  N  K  R  Y  E
K  I  T  L  E  H  S  T  D  B        K  S  T  G  E  D  S  G  D  T
I  C  F  P  B  U  A  N  D  A        I  W  U  H  B  E  A  M  D  N
N  S  P  A  I  N  T  E  D  R        F  E  L  T  O  D  B  A  Z  A
D  F  M  J  A  G  O  W  R  G        D  P  M  J  A  L  K  D  S  L
E  D  O  R  R  E  F  L  E  R        N  T  O  K  I  C  K  E  D  P
D  F  C  H  D  R  O  I  W  Y        O  D  E  S  S  A  P  A  I  V
```

rode	went	showed	planted
said	told	felt	made
painted	grabbed	ended	swept
hung	ate	blew	kicked
drew	mended **13**	brought	passed **14**

```
P  R  E  U  S  C  G  A  E  D        S  H  O  O  K  F  G  B  W  I
T  F  W  L  D  I  E  D  B  L        U  F  K  L  K  B  T  U  R  L
M  G  A  I  R  J  E  D  V  G        J  U  M  P  E  D  E  M  O  G
P  T  S  T  O  P  P  E  D  A        P  D  E  A  T  B  E  N  T  A
D  B  T  H  V  R  S  D  I  W        K  E  T  D  E  O  S  G  E  T
E  C  U  P  E  O  A  R  D  E        I  K  U  D  B  U  A  R  D  R
K  S  P  G  I  H  B  U  Z  R        N  O  P  L  O  G  B  R  Z  A
R  X  F  E  L  L  K  R  S  G        D  O  M  E  S  H  O  N  E  N
A  H  I  U  T  E  F  T  V  X        N  C  O  D  E  T  L  E  M  G
M  D  E  N  A  O  R  G  I  S        D  F  C  H  C  I  E  X  S  Z
```

groaned	saw	wrote	melted
did	stopped	bent	shone
added	fell	jumped	cooked
drove	grew	paddled	bought
marked	died **15**	rang	shook **16**

Kriss Kross Adverbs

Puzzle 17

```
U R Y A W A G B T Y
P S L I K B O X O L
M D L T A E U I M I
B R U J T S T R O P
I A F N O O S G R E
K W E P B O I U R E
Z K P H Y L D U O L
D C O J A L E R W S
N A H E R E H W O N
D B S Y A W E D I S
```

tomorrow	soon
loudly	backwards
sideways	away
outside	nowhere
sleepily	hopefully

17

Puzzle 18

```
S R E A R L Y B I R
U F K N K B M X G L
I T R Y A E O S E U
F O R W A R D S N Y
K D T H E R L G T L
I A U E B W E L L I
D Y P R O H S R Y S
O F M E J L K R S I
W H O U R E E C N O
N F C H D I J A X N
```

forwards	once
early	noisily
gently	well
anywhere	today
down	seldom

18

Puzzle 19

```
X S O M E T I M E S
U D F L V B N I T L
R G T U E Z S P A G
P T E J R S I M L Y
K A N H Y R D E B L
E L S E W H E R E K
N W P I H E B R I C
D A T H E R E I S I
N Y O U R E F L Y U
D S C F E R D Y M Q
```

there	often
sometimes	everywhere
always	late
quickly	merrily
elsewhere	inside

19

Puzzle 20

```
F A S T S F H G I H
M Y L E N O L X S Y
U L R W G E A M V A
P N E V E R T R Y D
T E T H I X E G A R
O D U P H E R E F E
N D P H O H B R T T
Q U I E T L Y R E S
N S O M E W H E R E
D F C H K R J A M Y
```

somewhere	here
never	later
quietly	fast
high	after
suddenly	yesterday

20

Kriss Kross Pronouns

```
G E Y A I U O Y T Y        I R E S R F Y B T R
E W L I K B U X O L        U F K N K B M X H L
M D T S A E R I M I        I T R H I M O S E U
X T H E M I T R O H        M O R E A R D S I Y
U A E N I L S R G I        E D T R E R L G R L
L D Y Z N U I E R S        I A U S B F E H S I
N K P H E E W H O L        D I P R O H S C Y S
S C O J A L K D H T        O T M E J L K I S I
H A B D F Y E H T N        W S O U R S E H E O
E B S Y A F E D I S        N F C S D I J W X N
```

her	she	me	he
mine	our	us	it
they	them	ours	I
his	who	which	hers
we	you	theirs	him

21
22

```
S U O M E G X H E B        F I T S S F W G I H
H D W H A T N I T U        U Y L E N O H I S I
E G T U E H E P S S        S L R W G E O M H M
P Y E J R E I M L Y        H N Y O U R S R M Y
I O N H Y I D E R L        E D T H I X E G A R
T X S E W R E W I K        I D U P H E R E I T
S F P I H E M E H T        N D M I N E B R T T
H A T S E R E I S Y        T J Y E T L E R E S
I Y O T R E F O Y O        T S O M E W H P I H
S P C I E R D W I U        D F C O U R S A M Y
```

what	she	mine	whose
us	its	his	its
you	their	ours	yours
them	we	it	my
her	his	him	she

23
24

Grammar Task Card: Nouns

1

1. Sort these nouns into two columns—PLACES and THINGS.

blanket   school   desert   fence   garden

door   street   soap   beach   candle

2. Fill in each space with a suitable noun.

a. We sailed out on the _____ in a small _____.

b. Wash your _____ and brush your _____.

c. A little _____ stood yapping at the _____.

d. My _____ has a new _____ and a new _____.

e. Lock the _____ with this _____.

Grammar Task Card: Nouns

2

1. Write these nouns in plural form.

a. pig   *d.* lemon   *g.* fox

b. rose   *e.* bench   *h.* calf

c. baby   *f.* boat   *i.* tooth

2. Give the proper nouns capital letters.

a. mr. baxter lives in sandgate.

b. jim's birthday is in july, and sam's is in april.

c. Our boat sailed down the colorado river and under london bridge.

d. Our friends from arizona visit us at christmas time.

e. The olympic games were held in beijing.

Grammar Task Card: Nouns

3

1. Write 10 compound words from the words below.

door	net	foot	slide	path	home	ball
run	land	mark	way	work	book	water

2. Add apostrophes to show possession.

a. an elephants trunk

b. the old mans beard

c. some birds beaks

d. someones hat

e. a dogs paws

f. our friends bikes

g. childrens books

h. a lizards skin

i. hens eggs

j. a pins head

Grammar Task Card: Nouns

4

1. Add "a," "an," or "the."

a. We have _____ olive tree in _____ yard.

b. _____ lady had _____ cup of coffee.

c. They saw _____ police car as they left _____ school.

d. I would like _____ apple and _____ orange.

e. _____ old man got on _____ bus.

2. Write the feminine form of these nouns.

a. king

b. stallion

c. gander

d. gentleman

e. uncle

f. man

g. bull

h. rooster

i. brother

j. prince

Grammar Task Card: Adjectives

1. **Place an adjective before the nouns.**
   a. He is wearing a _____ shirt.
   b. I like _____ apples and _____ grapes.
   c. On _____ days, we drive down to the beach.
   d. He stood beside the _____ wall.
   e. A camel is a _____ animal.

2. **Place an adjective after the noun.**
   a. The cows in the pasture are _____.
   b. The puppy is black and _____.
   c. The knives on the table are _____.
   d. She is so _____.
   e. An elephant is _____ and _____.

Grammar Task Card: Adjectives

1. **Sort these adjectives into two columns—describing PEOPLE or describing THINGS.**

   serious   plastic   wobbly   clever   wide   rich   helpful   crushed

   tin   worried   friendly useful lonely green brave   straw

2. **Choose an adjective below from the top line to describe a noun on the bottom line.**

   crackling   gardening   swimming   potted   melted   branded

   cows   plant   fire   ice   gloves   pool

3. **List the adjectives. Use them in sentences.**

   large   robot   salty   important   crunchy

   carton   exciting pasta   library   unusual

Grammar Task Card: Adjectives

3

1. List the adjectives in this story.

It was a cloudy, hot day. Dad said, "Let's go to the beach. It will be cooler there."

We drove there in Dad's new, red car. The sand was soft. The breeze was cool on our faces. The water was warm and refreshing. We all had a good time.

2. Fill in the gaps for these adjectives of degree.

a. _____ fatter fattest

b. happy _____ _____

c. _____ _____ safest

d. _____ older _____

Grammar Task Card: Adjectives

4

1. Write the antonyms of these words.

happy   young   stale   slow   long   narrow   bright
sour   heavy   safe   clean   weak   small   low

2. Fill in the gaps for these adjectives of degree.

a. high _____ _____

b. _____ angrier _____

c. _____ _____ cleanest

d. grand _____ _____

Grammar Task Card: Pronouns ①

1. Put in the correct pronoun—"I" or "me."

  a. Mom and _____ went to the supermarket.

  b. Dad gave Jasmine and _____ a dollar to spend.

  c. _____ didn't know you wanted to see _____.

  d. After school, Alex and _____ go skateboarding.

  e. Why don't you come with Alex and _____?

2. Choose the right word—"their" or "there."

  a. _____ were two dirty cups on the sink.

  b. They put _____ books on the teacher's table.

  c. Tell them to put _____ scraps in the trash.

  d. I opened the door but no one was _____.

  e. _____ was such a fuss when they left _____ hats on the bus.

Grammar Task Card: Pronouns ②

1. Rewrite these sentences, adding in the missing pronouns.

  a. She waited for _____ friend by the school gate.

  b. Dad went fishing with _____ friends.

  c. The twins bought a bunch of flowers for _____ mother.

  d. _____ like pizza.

  e. We called out to _____ as they came around the bend.

2. Begin these questions with "who," "which," "what," or "whose."

  a. _____ can make paper airplanes?

  b. _____ boys ride bikes to school?

  c. _____ would you like for lunch?

  d. _____ is the youngest person in the class?

  e. _____ jacket is this?

Grammar Task Card: Pronouns

3

1. Add a possessive pronoun to these sentences.

   a. Did you find _____ lost dog?

   b. I think that water bottle is _____.

   c. Jacob put on _____ helmet and went out to bat.

   d. We lost _____ way in the rain forest.

   e. Ah, that's _____. Please give it back.

   f. In winter I wear _____ flannel pajamas.

   g. Mom told my sister and me to clean _____ rooms.

2. Use the correct pronoun to complete the sentences.

   a. (They Them) took us to the beach.

   b. The kitten is licking (it its) paws.

   c. (Her She) had a haircut this afternoon.

   d. Would (you your) like to come to the movies with me?

   e. (Him He) told his son to buy the paper.

Grammar Task Card: Pronouns

4

1. Use these pronouns in sentences.

we	mine	they	us
your	it	her	our

2. What nouns do the underlined pronouns replace?

   a. "Do <u>you</u> want to go for a walk, Josh?" asked Andy.

   b. "Show <u>me</u> your paintings," said the teacher.

   c. Priya said to Brianna, "<u>I</u> will call you soon."

   d. The children shouted, "Wait for <u>us</u>."

   e. "Will you take <u>my</u> picture?" Marty asked Mia.

   f. "Put <u>your</u> hands on <u>your</u> head," the coach said to his team.

Grammar Task Card: Verbs

1

1. Fill in the sentences with "did" or "done."

TIP: "Done" always needs a helper. (I <u>did</u> my work. I <u>have done</u> my work.)

a. We _____ our homework.

b. They have _____ a good job.

c. I have not _____ anything wrong.

d. _____ you see the tiny possum?

e. The artist _____ some painting.

f. Have you _____ all your chores?

g. We knew he had _____ it.

h. Has she _____ her homework?

2. Fill in the sentences with "went" or "gone."

TIP: "Gone" always needs a helper. (She <u>went</u> to school. She <u>has</u> <u>gone</u> to school.)

a. He _____ to the movies.

b. They have _____ for a walk.

c. Has she _____ with them?

d. Tom _____ by plane to Paris.

e. I _____ to see Uncle Bert.

f. Have they _____ yet?

g. We _____ to bed early.

h. Where have they _____?

Grammar Task Card: Verbs

2

1. Fill in the sentences with "saw" or "seen."

TIP: "Seen" always needs a helper. (They <u>saw</u> the movie. They <u>have seen</u> the movie.)

a. I _____ you climbing that tree.

b. Have you _____ my kitten?

c. He _____ me on the bus.

d. She has _____ the movie twice.

e. You _____ the deer, didn't you?

f. We _____ where you lived.

g. Has he _____ your new bike?

h. I don't know who you _____.

2. List only the verbs.

speak   plastic   stir   sneeze   nasty   bite   funny   drive

gold   drip   have   seize   after   lonely   sleep   build

Grammar Task Card: Verbs

3

1. Rewrite these sentences in the past tense.

a. We <u>buy</u> candles.

b. They <u>wear</u> hats.

c. We often <u>see</u> them.

d. I <u>bend</u> down.

e. He <u>stands</u> up tall.

f. They <u>sit</u> on chairs.

g. I <u>pat</u> my cat.

h. I <u>dry</u> the dishes.

i. They <u>walk</u> in the park.

j. We <u>wave</u> goodbye.

2. Write these negative verbs as contractions.

a. did not

b. could not

c. has not

d. cannot

e. is not

f. would not

g. will not

h. was not

i. are not

j. have not

k. do not

l. were not

Grammar Task Card: Verbs

4

1. Add the correct ending to the verb—"–ing" or "–ed."

One afternoon, a boy and his dog were walk____ along the beach. The boy was look____ for shells. He was carry____ a bucket and a shovel. The dog was trot____ happily along at the boy's heels.

Then a large wave roll____ up the beach. The dog bark____. Off went the boy, run____ and splash____ through the water. He pick____ up the shells, before they could be wash____ away again.

2. Write these pronouns and verbs as contractions.

a. she will

b. they have

c. you are

d. he is

e. we are

f. I would

g. they are

h. he would

i. she has

j. we would

k. I am

l. we will

Grammar Task Card: Adverbs

1. **Add an adverb of manner (how) to say more about the verb.**

   a. We clapped _____ at the end of the show.

   b. We walked _____ up the steep hill.

   c. A shark glided _____ through the water.

   d. Who is that knocking so _____ on the door?

   e. The bike riders rode _____ in the race.

2. **List the adverbs in these sentences.**

   a. The wind blew strongly.

   b. She fell backwards into the pool.

   c. He climbed up and up and up.

   d. We will join you at the park later.

   e. The train went faster and faster.

Grammar Task Card: Adverbs

1. **Change these adjectives to adverbs. Watch your spelling.**

   a. large   *c.* grand   *e.* narrow   *g.* famous   *i.* soft

   b. steady   *d.* late   *f.* lazy   *h.* joyful   *j.* happy

2. **Complete the questions, using the adverbs "how," "when," "where," or "why."**

   a. _____ do panda bears live?

   b. _____ far can you throw this ball?

   c. _____ did you go to your grandma's?

   d. _____ are you late?

   e. _____ will I find a book about possums?

Grammar Task Card: Adverbs

3

1. Use the correct word in the parentheses.

a. Rain fell (heavy heavily) on the roof.

b. Ken walked (wary wearily) back home.

c. You will catch the bus if you are (quick quickly).

d. Don't handle your pets (rough roughly).

e. You acted (bad badly).

2. Write sentences using these adverbs.

here	never	sleepily
backwards	later	why

Grammar Task Card: Adverbs

4

1. What do the adverbs tell us—how, when, or where?

a. I go for a run <u>early</u> in the morning.

b. She sat <u>quietly</u> with her mother.

c. I couldn't find my kitten <u>anywhere</u>.

d. <u>Tomorrow</u> we are going to make clay dinosaurs.

e. The fox eyed the hens <u>hungrily</u>.

2. Name the verbs that the adverbs say more about.

a. He crept <u>forward</u> and hid behind a tree.

b. The building blocks all fell <u>down</u>.

c. The children chattered <u>excitedly</u>.

d. If you leave <u>tomorrow</u>, I'll come with you.

e. I <u>often</u> buy an ice-cream cone at the shop.

Grammar Task Card: Sentences
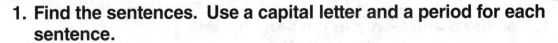

1

1. Find the sentences. Use a capital letter and a period for each sentence.

    Sammy went to visit his Aunt Nell at her little beach house he had a room upstairs overlooking the water Sammy and his aunt swam every day they gathered seaweed and shells Aunt Nell's dog was always nearby

2. A sentence always has a verb. Pick out the verbs in these sentences.

   a. They played baseball in the backyard.

   b. The sun glittered on the white snow.

   c. Rain fell heavily.

   d. The baby sits in a high chair.

   e. The people are skiing down the mountain.

Grammar Task Card: Sentences

2

1. Write a subject for each sentence.

   a. _____ ran towards the open gate.

   b. _____ lost his map and compass.

   c. On the floor lay _____.

   d. Up the steep hill went _____.

   e. _____ put three dollars in his bank.

2. Here are some subjects. Add a predicate (the rest of the sentence).

   a. Many children _____.

   b. The helicopter _____.

   c. All the people _____.

   d. Wild horses _____.

   e. The farmer _____.

Grammar Task Card: Sentences

3

1. Join the two sentences to make one compound sentence. Use the joining words "and," "but," or "so."

a.	I like apples.	Paul likes plums.
b.	It is late.	I must leave.
c.	I ate a cupcake.	I drank a glass of milk.
d.	We would like to stay.	We have to catch a train.
e.	He stood up.	He could be seen.

2. Join the predicates to their correct subjects.

a.	The boy at the desk	spun a large web.
b.	My yellow kite	eat eggs for breakfast.
c.	Every morning, I	was writing a story.
d.	The black spider	fell and cut her knee.
e.	In the race, Jessie	hit the top of a tree.

Grammar Task Card: Sentences

4

1. Punctuate these sentences.

a. we went to the airport to watch the planes

b. have you been to the zoo to see the crocodiles

c. you're in trouble

d. collect the eggs from the henhouse, please

e. will you play chess with me

2. Punctuate these pieces of dialogue.

happy birthday Liz said her mom handing her a little box

oh thank you mom she replied opening her gift this is beautiful she said holding up the gold necklace

have you seen my kitten Mrs Johns asked Toby

Mrs Johns replied yes I just saw her jump the back fence

WORD BANK

Antonyms
Opposites

ADJECTIVES

awake	*asleep*
black	*white*
bright	*dull*
clean	*dirty*
cold	*hot*
dear	*cheap*
expensive	*cheap*
far	*near*
fast	*slow*
fat	*thin*
fat	*lean*
fresh	*stale*
full	*empty*
great	*small*
high	*low*
ill	*well*
kind	*unkind*
light	*dark*
light	*heavy*
little	*big*
long	*short*
old	*new*
old	*young*
right	*wrong*
right	*left*
sad	*happy*
small	*large*
smooth	*rough*
smooth	*coarse*
soft	*hard*
soft	*loud*
top	*bottom*
ugly	*beautiful*
wet	*dry*
wide	*narrow*
wild	*tame*

VERBS

open	*shut*	win	*lose*
come	*go*	stand	*sit*
ebb	*flow*	sleep	*wake*
sink	*float*	open	*close*
throw	*catch*	stop	*go*

NOUNS

morning	*afternoon*	dawn	*dusk*
day	*night*	friend	*foe*
love	*hate*	life	*death*

ADVERBS

late	*early*	now	*then*
sooner	*later*	often	*seldom*

PREPOSITIONS

up	*down*	behind	*ahead*
above	*below*	over	*under*
after	*before*	in	*out*
off	*on*	with	*without*

afternoon	eggplant	inside	quarterback
anthill	eggshell	jumpstart	quarter-time
armchair	eyebrow	junkyard	railway/railroad
backside	eyelash	kick-boxer	rainbow/raindrops
bandstand	eyeliner	landslide/landline	raincoat
barnyard	failsafe	leeway	rosebud
baseball	fairway	lifeline/lifetime	sandbag
basketball	fairytale	lighthouse	sandcastle
bathroom	farmland	lightweight	scarecrow
bedroom/bedtime	farmyard	lunchbox	shockproof
bellboy	fingernail	manhole	shoelace/shoestring
birthday	fireball/firefly	manpower	showtime
blackboard	firelight/fireplace	matchbox	skylight
bookcase	fireman/firestorm	matchstick	slipstream/slipway
bookends	fireproof	merry-go-round	snowball/snowflake
bookmark	foolhardy	milkman	snowman
bridegroom	football	milkshake	softball
broomstick	footbridge/footloose	moonlight/moonbeam	starlight/starburst
bulldozer	footpath/footprint	mothballs	steamroller
bullseye	fullback	mudpie	stopwatch
buttercup	gentleman	nevermore	sunbeam/sunburst
buttermilk	goalkeeper	nickname	sunlight/sunshine
butterscotch	godmother/godfather	nightdress	tablecloth
cardboard	grandmother/grandfather	nightfall	teapot
catfish	grandstand	nighttime	telltale
carthorse	grapefruit	nursemaid	timeline
cartwheel	grapevine	offside	timepiece
cornflakes	halfback	outpost	toenail
cowboy/cowgirl	handbag	outside	toothpaste/toothbrush
daybreak	handheld	overall	topside
daydream	handlebar	overeat	towbar
daylight	handmade	overlap	toyshop
daytime	handstand	overstay	washstand
dipstick	haystack	overtime	watchmaker
doorknob/doorknock	headlight/headstand	paperweight	waterbed/watermelon
doorbell	heartbeat/heartfelt	pathway	watercolor/waterway
doorstep	herself/himself	penknife	watercourse/waterproof
doorstop	hillside	pickpocket	waterfront/watercress
doorway	homeland	pigsty	watertight
downhearted	homesick	pinwheel	watermark/waterfall
downhill	homestead	playtime/playhouse	waterworks
downstairs	horseback/horseplay	policeman	waxworks
downstream	horsehair/horseshoe	popcorn	weekend/weekday
downtown	hornpipe	porthole	whirlwind
downtrodden	houseboat	postcard	windmill
drainpipe	household	postman	witchcraft
driveway	inland/inlet	pothole	

ail/ale
air/heir
aisle/isle/I'll
allowed/aloud
alter/altar
arc/ark
ascent/assent
ate/eight
aunt/ant
bail/bale
bald/bawled
bare/bear
barren/baron
base/bass
be/bee
beach/beech
bell/belle
berry/bury
birth/berth
blew/blue
boar/bore
board/bored
boarder/border
bold/bowled
born/borne
bough/bow
bow/beau
braid/brayed
braise/brays
brake/break
bread/bred
brews/bruise
bridal/bridle
but/butt
buy/by/bye
cannon/canon
canvas/canvass
capital/capitol
carrot/carat
cast/caste
cede/seed
ceiling/sealing
cellar/seller
cent/scent/sent
cents/scents/sense
cereal/serial

cheap/cheep
check/cheque
chews/chose
choral/coral
cite/sight/site
clause/claws
coarse/course
coat/cote
colonel/kernel
core/corps
council/counsel
creak/creek
crews/cruise
curb/kerb
currant/current
cygnet/signet
days/daze
dear/deer
dew/due
die/dye
died/dyed
dies/dyes
doe/dough
dying/dyeing
earn/urn
ewe/you/yew
ewes/use
eye/I
eyelet/islet
faint/feint
fair/fare
feat/feet
find/fined
fir/fur
flea/flee
flew/flu/flue
flocks/phlox
flow/floe
flower/flour
for/fore/four
foul/fowl
frays/phrase
freeze/frieze
gait/gate
gamble/gambol
genes/jeans

gild/guild
gored/gourd
gorilla/guerrilla
grate/great
groan/grown
guest/guessed
hail/hale
hanger/hangar
hart/heart
heal/heel/he'll
hear/here
heard/herd
hears/here's
hew/hue
higher/hire
him/hymn
ho/hoe
hoard/horde
hoarse/horse
hose/hoes
hole/whole
holy/wholly
hour/our
idle/idol
in/inn
knead/need/kneed
knew/new
knight/night
knot/not
know/no
knows/nose
lacks/lax
lain/lane
laps/lapse
lead/led
leak/leek
lessen/lesson
liar/lyre
licence/license
lieu/Lou
lightening/lightning
links/lynx
load/lode
loan/lone
loot/lute
made/maid

mail/male
main/mane
maize/maze
mall/maul
manner/manor
mantel/mantle
mare/mayor
marshal/martial
meat/meet/mete
medal/meddle
metal/mettle
metre/meter
might/mite
mined/mind
miner/minor
missed/mist
moan/mown
moat/mote
mode/mowed
more/moor
morn/mourn
morning/mourning
muscle/mussel
mustard/mustered
nay/neigh
none/nun
ode/owed
one/won
or/oar/ore
paced/paste
packed/pact
pail/pale
pain/pane
pair/pare/pear
passed/past
patience/patients
poor/pore
peace/piece
peak/peek
peer/pier
pedal/peddle

WORD BANK   Collective Nouns

a brood of chickens

a business of ferrets

a cloud of flies

a clutch of eggs

a flock of birds

a gaggle of geese

a herd of buffalo

a herd of elephants

a litter of cubs

a mob of cattle

a murder of cows

a pack of dogs

a rake of colts

a school of fish

a shrewdness of apes

a siege of herons

a skulk of foxes

a sloth of bears

a swarm of bees

an army of frogs

a convoy of trucks

a flock of sheep

a kindle of kittens

a leap of leopards

a mob of kangaroos

a pack of wolves

a parliament of owls

a pod of whales

a pride of lions

a rafter of turkeys

a school of porpoises

a smack of jellyfish

a string of racehorses

a team of horses

a tiding of magpies

a troop of monkeys

a warren of rabbits

a watch of nightingales

a wedge of swans

an exaltation of larks

SPELLING RULES and Generalizations

ADDING WORD ENDINGS

Words ending in "e"

<u>Drop</u> the "e" before adding an ending that begins with a vowel.

e.g., bite, biting; fame, famous; slime, slimy

<u>Keep</u> the "e" if adding an ending which begins with a consonant.

e.g., spite, spiteful; state, statement; safe, safety

Words ending in "y"

<u>Change</u> the "y" to "i" if the letter before the "y" is a consonant.

e.g., happy, happiness; busy, business; beauty, beautiful; primary, primarily

<u>Keep</u> the "y" if the letter before the "y" is a vowel.

e.g., play, playful; destroy, destroyed; employ, employment

Doubling Rule

When a syllable contains a short vowel followed by one consonant, that consonant is usually doubled before adding an ending.

e.g., hit, hitting; sun, sunny; fat, fatter; cat, cattle; shut, shutter

Verbs ending in "c"

Add a "k" to words ending in "c" before adding "ing" or "ed."

e.g., panic, panicking; picnic, picnicked

Verbs ending in "l"

Double the "l" before adding "ing" or "ed."

e.g., quarrel, quarrelling; patrol, patrolled

Words ending in "le"

Drop the "le" before adding the "ly."

e.g., subtle, subtly; simple, simply

Words ending in "ge" or "ve"

Keep the "e" before adding suffixes such as "ous" or "able."

e.g., manage, manageable; outrage, outrageous; move, moveable

Words ending in "d" or "de"

Change the "d" or "de" to an "s" before adding the suffix "ion."

e.g., suspend, suspension; apprehend, apprehension; decide, decision; conclude, conclusion

Apostrophe of Contraction

An apostrophe is used to indicate the place where a letter or letters have been omitted when two words are contracted.

e.g., could not, couldn't; I will, I'll

Soft "c"

When "c" is followed by "e," "i," or "y," it is usually sounded as an "s."

e.g., city, cent, cycle

Capital Letters

Proper nouns, or adjectives formed from proper nouns, begin with capital letters.

e.g., America, American; Italy, Italian

Soft "g"

When "g" is followed by "e," "i," or "y," it is usually sounded as a "j."

e.g., gentle, giant, gym, engine, agent

Some exceptions: girl, get

SPELLING RULES and Generalizations

Apostrophe of Possession

An apostrophe is used to show possession by a person, animal, or thing.

Singular Nouns

Add "s" to the end (even if the word already ends in "s").

e.g., this girl's hat; the cat's whiskers; Ross's boots

Plural Nouns

If the word already ends in "s," just add an apostrophe.

e.g., these students' books; the parents' decision; rabbits' ears

If the plural form does not end in "s," add "s."

e.g., children's parties; sheep's wool; those deer's antlers

General Rule—"ie" or "ei"

It is helpful to remember that "i" comes before "e" except after "c."

e.g., chief, shield, niece, receive, deceit, conceive

Exception: ancient

General Rule—Writing Numbers

Write numbers below 10 in words.

e.g., seven, eight, six

Use a hyphen between numbers containing tens and ones.

e.g., ninety-five, sixty-one

ADDING WORD ENDINGS

Plurals are usually formed by adding "s" or "es" to the noun.

Add "es" to words ending in "sh," "ch," "s," "ss," "x," "z," "zz" and some words ending in "o."

There are many irregular plurals.

e.g., tooth, teeth; child, children

Words ending in "y"

If the letter before the "y" is a vowel, add "s."

e.g., key, keys; valley, valleys

If the letter before the "y" is a consonant, change the "y" to "i" and add "es."

e.g., lady, ladies; body, bodies; balcony, balconies

Words ending in "f" or "fe"

Change the "f" to "v" and add "es."

e.g., knife, knives; leaf, leaves; wolf, wolves

Some exceptions: roofs, chiefs, hoofs, waifs

Words ending in "eu" or "eau"

These words have been imported from the French language. Plurals are formed by adding "x."

e.g., adieu, adieux; milieu, milieux; gateau, gateaux; plateau, plateaux

Same form

Some nouns are spelled the same in both their singular and plural form.

e.g., fish, sheep, deer, squid, salmon

Plurals—words that are always plural

Many nouns only have a plural form.

e.g., scissors, trousers, cattle, pants, police, clothes

Compound Nouns

The plural is sometimes formed by adding "s" within the structure of the word.

e.g., mother-in-law, mothers-in-law

A word about PUNCTUATION

Capital letters are used for:

EXAMPLE:

- the first word in a sentence.

  Come to the circus with me.

- proper names.

  Cinderella danced with Prince Charming.

- the first spoken word in dialogue.

  He said, "Let's play baseball."

- to emphasize important words.

  You did WHAT?

Periods end statements and commands.

That is a fine straw hat.
Put it on, please.

Question marks end questions.

How long will you be away?

Exclamation marks end exclamations.

What! Late again!

Commas are used:

- to separate words in a list.

  I like apples, pears, plums, and grapes.

- to separate a beginning phrase.

  Later that day, we went for a swim.

- to separate a beginning clause.

  When I broke my leg, I used crutches.

- to separate an embedded phrase.

  Jess, waving her umbrella, hurried away.

- to separate an embedded clause.

  My dog, which is old now, still does tricks.

- to separate spoken and unspoken words.

  "A dingo is a wild dog," said Bradley.

Quotation marks are used around spoken words.

"Dinner is on the table," called Brenda.
"Thank you," Jess replied.
Remember: NEW speaker NEW lines.

Apostrophes are used:

- with nouns to show possession.

  Joel's toys; dog's collar; teacher's lunchroom

- to contract pronouns and helping verbs.

  I've packed lunch. You're invited. It's fun.

- to contract helping verbs and negatives.

  He can't swim. I couldn't sing. Don't shout.

NOUNS

Student Page 1 (page 19)
1. Answers will vary.

Student Page 2 (page 20)
1. Answers will vary.
2. a. bus   c. boy, bat
   b. flowers, teacher   (Check drawings.)
3. house, apple, parrot or bird

Student Page 3 (page 21)
1. a. koala   c. dentist
   b. soccer   d. sandwiches

2.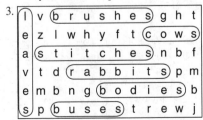

3. Answers will vary.

Student Page 4 (page 22)
1. a. apples   d. boxes
   b. monkeys   e. dishes
   c. spoons   f. scratches
2. a. girls, ribbons
   b. books, boxes
   c. keys, cushions
   d. pears, oranges, bananas, peaches
   e. buses, passengers

Student Page 5 (page 23)
1. a. countries   d. daisies, pansies
   b. ladies, keys   e. gullies
   c. donkeys
2. a. wolves   d. calves
   b. knives   e. loaves
   c. leaves

Student Page 6 (page 24)
1. a. tooth, teeth   d. foot, feet
   b. goose, geese   e. woman, women
   c. man, men   f. child, children
2. a. The children went with the ladies.
   b. The autumn leaves fell onto the red roofs.
   c. My sisters ate the peaches in the dishes.
3. (word search)

Student Page 7 (page 25)
1. a. Anthony, Chicago, Cottonwood Elementary School
   b. Saturday, March

   c. Christmas, Hawaii
   d. David, T-mart
   e. Kim, Germany, World Cup
2. a. Disneyland, June
   b. Jack's, Harry Potter
   c. Shymal, India, Texas
   d. New York, Statue of Liberty
3. Answers will vary.

Student Page 8 (page 26)
1. a. haystack   d. bedroom
   b. kickboxing   e. football
   c. toothbrush
2. a. grandstand   d. cornflakes
   b. sunshine   e. broomstick
   c. waterfall   f. hillside
3. Answers will vary.

Student Page 9 (page 27)
1. a. Harry's   d. Priya's
   b. Tegan's   e. Mom's
   c. Dylan's
2. a. brother's   d. teacher's
   b. Maria's   e. parrot's
   c. sailor's
3. Answers will vary.
4. Check drawings.

Student Page 10 (page 28)
1. a. more than one   d. more than one
   b. more than one   e. one
   c. one
2. a. horses'   d. swimmers'
   b. cups'   e. eagle's
   c. car's
3. a. lions'   d. teachers'
   b. elephants'   e. cousins'
   c. crocodiles'

Student Page 11 (page 29)
1. bull/cow, man/woman, ram/ewe, king/queen, uncle/aunt, stallion/mare
2. Check drawings.
3. teacher, athlete, doctor, poet, instructor, thief

Student Page 12 (page 30)
1. a. a black mountain bike
   b. A mean, old fox
   c. the sweet plums
   d. A big gray seagull
   e. The strong elephant
   f. a new green jacket
2. a. an interesting television show
   b. The black and white magpie
   c. a box of chocolates
   d. a box of cornflakes, a bottle of milk
3. Answers will vary.

Student Page 13 (page 31)
1. a. children, ride, Ferris wheel
   b. horse, pasture
   c. boy, birds
   d. pool, hour
   e. girl, cookie, orange
2. a. an, a   d. an, a
   b. a, an, a   e. an
   c. an

3. a. a, the   d. the, the
   b. The, a, the   e. a
   c. the, a

Assessment—Nouns (pages 32 and 33)
1. Jamie, soldiers, coats, pants, box
2. a. benches   d. games
   b. clocks   e. leaves
   c. ladies
3. a. girl's   d. kids'
   b. fishermen's   e. Katie's
   c. cat's
4. a. the   c. The, a
   b. a   d. an
5. Answers will vary: lighthouse, farmhouse, playhouse, playtime, lifetime, lifeline, daytime, timeline, sunlight
6. a. Townsville
   b. Jordan
   c. Easter
   d. France, September
7. princess/prince, man/woman, rooster/hen, mother/father, bull/cow
8. Answers will vary.

ADJECTIVES

Student Page 14 (page 37)
1. Answers will vary.
2. a. busy   e. tall
   b. sweet   f. fat
   c. sly   g. long
   d. pretty
3. Answers will vary.

Student Page 15 (page 38)
1. a. round, juicy, sweet
   b. heavy, interesting, thick
   c. flowering, leafy, green
   d. soft, playful, furry
   e. cheese, fresh, tasty
2. a. patient, kind   d. chocolate
   b. playful   e. noisy
   c. tired
3. a. school   d. tin
   b. large   e. faithful
   c. boat

Student Page 16 (page 39)
1. Answers will vary.
2. Answers will vary.

Student Page 17 (page 40)
1. a. two, two, two   e. many
   b. eight   f. some or many
   c. two, two, four   g. few
   d. six
2. Color: brown, orange, purple, yellow, scarlet; Size: small, large, huge, enormous, tiny; Shape: round, circular, triangular, oval, square

Student Page 18 (page 41)
1. a. dirty   d. stale
   b. low   e. big
   c. wide   f. long, tall

ANSWER KEY

2. a. dirty   d. big
   b. low   e. long
   c. narrow   f. stale
3. a. fast   e. light
   b. short   f. rough
   c. low   g. old
   d. happy   h. hard

```
S  L  P (H  A  R) D
D (O  L  D) X  O  L
(T  W  G  Y  P  U  Q
 S  H  O  R  T) G  Z
 A (Y  P  P  A  H) R
 F) S (L  I  G  H  T)
```

Student Page 19 (page 42)

1. a. racing bikes   d. roasted peanuts
   b. waiting room   e. buttered bread
   c. interesting books f. baked beans
2. Answers will vary.
3. Check drawings.

Student Page 20 (page 43)

1. short, shorter, shortest; safe, safer, safest; wet, wetter, wettest; low, lower, lowest; large, larger, largest
2. long, longer, longest; old, older, oldest; sharp, sharper, sharpest; wild, wilder, wildest; soft, softer, softest; brave, braver, bravest
3. a. smaller   c. youngest
   b. fastest   d. older

Assessment—Adjectives (pages 44 and 45)

1. a. lost
   b. first
   c. scrambled, boiled
   d. seven, round
   e. new, blue, white
   f. flowering
2. a. dancing shoes g. loaded truck
   b. cooking pots   h. parked cars
   c. building blocks i. whipped cream
   d. chewing gum j. grated cheese
   e. walking stick k. potted plant
   f. setting sun   l. grilled fish
3. a. larger   d. longer
   b. hottest   e. thick
   c. slowest
4. Answers will vary.
5. Answers will vary.
6. a. apple   c. desert
   b. ball   d. tree

PRONOUNS

Student Page 21 (page 49)

1. a. me   d. them
   b. I, him   e. We, our
   c. She, her
2. a. Ned, bird
   b. cats, mice
   c. Lynn, hat
   d. the reader, Tom and the reader, kittens
   e. the children, apples
3. a. her   d. them
   b. They   e. him
   c. He, it

Student Page 22 (page 50)

1. a. they
   b. he, it
   c. She, it
   d. I (he, she, we), them
   e. We (I, They)
2. Masculine: he, him; Feminine: her, she; Plural: they, we, us, them
3. Answers will vary.

Student Page 23 (page 51)

1. a. her   d. me, mine
   b. His, him e. They, their
   c. yours
2. Suggested answers:
   a. our   d. my
   b. hers   e. his, his
   c. their   f. your
3.

```
(T  H  E  I  R  S) F (S
 J (M (Y  O  U  R) L  I
 I  I  O  U  R  S) G  H
 M  N  U  D  A (O  U  R)
(H  E  R) (T  H  E  I  R)
 Z  X (S  M (H  E  R  S)
```

Student Page 24 (page 52)

1. a. hers   c. theirs
   b. our   d. my, mine
2. a. He   e. She
   b. It   f. I
   c. her   g. it
   d. her   h. his

Student Page 25 (page 53)

1. Answers will vary.
2. a. Whose   c. Which
   b. What   d. Who
3. a. Who went to the beach for their vacation?
   b. Whose house is made of brick?
   c. Which sport do you play in the summer?
   d. What did you eat for dinner last night?

Student Page 26 (page 54)

1. Suggested answers:
   a. everyone
   b. none
   c. anyone/anybody
   d. someone/somebody
   e. few
   f. some
2. a. that   d. those
   b. This   e. those, these
   c. these   f. This

Assessment—Pronouns (page 55)

1. a. She, him   d. you, we
   b. I, my   e. It, their
   c. They, her
2. his, They, they, their, her, them, she, You, you, they
3. a. He—Nuno, them—silkworms
   b. They—cats, them—birds
   c. She—May-Lin, it—dress
   d. They—Ted and Jeff, them—kittens
   e. We—Robbie and I, it—puppy

4. Make sure all pronouns are included in the sentences.

VERBS

Student Page 27 (page 59)

1. a. farmer/planted
   b. bike riders/raced
   c. dancer/twirls
   d. class/went
   e. They/jump
   f. teacher/counted
   g. I/cooked
2. a. no   e. no
   b. yes   f. yes
   c. no   g. yes/no
   d. no   h. yes/no

Student Page 28 (page 60)

1. a. bounced
   b. rang, answered
   c. read
   d. made
   e. landed
2. Answers will vary.
3. a. wag
   b. swim
   c. hunt
   d. play
   e. lay
   f. clap/wash/wave/etc.
   g. paint/draw
   h. falls
   i. fly
   j. clean/brush
   k. drive
   l. ride

Student Page 29 (page 61)

1. a. ask   d. explained
   b. say   e. cried
   c. talk   f. gasped
2. Answers will vary.
3. Answers will vary.

Student Page 30 (page 62)

1. a. Have   e. had
   b. has or had f. have or had
   c. have or had g. have
   d. have or had h. has
2. a. am   f. be
   b. are   g. were
   c. was   h. is/was
   d. been   i. being
   e. is, was j. been

Student Page 31 (page 63)

1. a. has   d. was, were
   b. had   e. am, are
   c. is, is
2. a. are/were c. have/had
   b. is/was   d. is/was
3. a. eaten   d. been
   b. waiting e. running
   c. writing

Student Page 32 (page 64)
1. a. are/were   d. Did
   b. has/had   e. will/shall, can/may
   c. will/shall/might   or did, could
2. Answers will vary.
3. Answers will vary.

Student Page 33 (page 65)
1. Answers will vary.
2. a. Mr. Jones does not have a new car.
   b. The miner has not gone down into the coal mine.
   c. We are not going to the beach.
   d. I cannot come with you tomorrow.
   e. She was not swimming in the lake.
3. Posters will vary.

Student Page 34 (page 66)
1. doesn't/does not, won't/will not, hadn't/had not, weren't/were not, didn't/did not, wouldn't/would not, can't/cannot, wasn't/was not, haven't/have not, aren't/are not, don't/do not, couldn't/could not
2. a. wouldn't/would not
   b. hasn't/has not
   c. didn't/did not
   d. weren't/were not
   e. haven't/have not
3. a. Sam couldn't swim well.
   b. We won't be singing in the choir.
   c. They haven't bought a pizza.
   d. Her hair hasn't been cut.
   e. Jilly isn't playing hockey today.

Student Page 35 (page 67)
1. a. The children
   b. We
   c. Many of my friends
   d. A soft gray koala
   e. Ben and I
2. a. The snakes slide.
   b. The birds sing.
   c. The doors are open.
   d. The boys have freckles.
   e. My cats like milk.
   f. The dogs were barking.
   g. They walk to school.
   h. We are hungry.

Student Page 36 (page 68)
1. I'll/I will, he's/he is, they've/they have, we're/we are, she'd/she would, you've/you have; I'm/I am, you're/you are, they're/they are, it's/it is, he'll/he will, we've/we have, you'll/you will, he'd/he would, she's/she is, they'd/they would, we'll/we will
2. a. You're   c. its
   b. We're   d. They're

Student Page 37 (page 69)
1. a. They've = They have
   b. he's = he is
   c. They'll = They will; it's = it is
   d. I'm = I am, you're = you are
   e. He'll = He will, they're = they are
   f. You'll = You will, we've = we have
2. a. Who is   c. I am, that is
   b. What is   d. Who has

Student Page 38 (page 70)
1. a. past   d. present
   b. present   e. past
   c. future   f. future
2. Check drawings.

Student Page 39 (page 71)
1. a. puffing   i. leaving
   b. reading   j. sliding
   c. teaching   k. stopping
   d. rolling   l. chatting
   e. bleeding   m. tugging
   f. chasing   n. nodding
   g. bouncing   o. gripping
   h. riding
2. Answers will vary.
3. Answers will vary.

Student Page 40 (page 72)
1. a. helped   i. lived
   b. rained   j. faded
   c. started   k. planned
   d. watched   l. stopped
   e. called   m. pinned
   f. shared   n. robbed
   g. closed   o. grinned
   h. changed
2. a. started
   b. watched
   c. shared
   d. called
   e. stopped, robbed
3. a. ate   g. grew
   b. gave   h. did
   c. spent   i. ran
   d. dug   j. had
   e. was   k. stood
   f. sang   l. broke

Student Page 41 (page 73)
1. Answers will vary.
2. Check drawings.
3. a. past   f. present
   b. present   g. past
   c. future   h. present
   d. future   i. future
   e. past

Assessment—Verbs (pages 74 and 75)
1. a. saved   d. have drifted
   b. was holding   e. will see
   c. Come
2. a. couldn't   d. Didn't
   b. He's   e. You're
   c. What's
3. a. are   d. are
   b. were   e. were
   c. am
4. a. grew   d. shook
   b. carried   e. was
   c. hopped
5. a. saw   d. seen
   b. seen   e. seen
   c. saw
6. a. moves   d. tries
   b. chew   e. drive
   c. have

7. a. shouted, yelled, said
   b. cried, groaned, said
   c. pleaded, begged, said
   d. grunted, growled, said
   e. moaned, groaned, muttered, said
8. a. Jack did all his homework.
   b. What have you done with all my marbles?
   c. They could not have done that without you.
   d. He asked Chen what he did for a living.
   e. Have you done as you were told?

ADVERBS

Student Page 42 (page 79)
1. a. how   d. when
   b. when   e. how
   c. where
2. a. loudly   d. here
   b. today   e. now, later
   c. quietly   f. away
3. Answers will vary.

Student Page 43 (page 80)
1. Suggested answers:
   a. loudly   d. wearily, quietly
   b. yesterday   e. backwards
   c. there, here   f. sometimes, often
2.

```
D T Y E N T O D A Y
O F S G J U B K L A
W G E D I S T U O W
N P M V D D H J R A
Q H I X L R G K Z I
L A T E R A I N P F
E V E R Y W H E R E
K O M W E R Y N C B
H U O J D O F T E N
T R S N U F L Y Z B
```

Student Page 44 (page 81)
1. a. fast, quickly   d. down
   b. loudly   e. north
   c. tomorrow, soon
2. a. He crept silently up the stairs.
   b. I spoke loudly, so everyone could hear.
   c. He pushed hard and the door opened.
   d. She arrived early and had to wait.
   e. It rained heavily for many days.
   f. They traveled north from Miami.
3. Answers will vary.

Student Page 45 (page 82)
1. a. clear, clearly
   b. sweet, sweetly
   c. dangerous, dangerously
   d. silent, silently
   e. simple, simply
   f. excited, excitedly
   g. foolish, foolishly
   h. careful, carefully
   i. kind, kindly
   j. busy, busily

ANSWER KEY

2. a. loudly   d. simple
   b. wisely   e. quietly
   c. badly
3. a. hastily   d. noisily
   b. happily   e. angrily
   c. greedily

Student Page 46 (page 83)

1. a. Where, When   d. When
   b. Why   e. Why
   c. How   f. How
2. Answers will vary.
3. a. Why are the children laughing?
   b. When is the final football game?
   c. How do you like your new bike?
   d. Where can I buy a pet rabbit?

Assessment—Adverbs (page 84 and 85)

1. a. where   d. when
   b. when   e. where
   c. how   f. how
2. steadily, early, brightly, soon, awhile
3. a. happily   f. weakly
   b. steeply   g. strongly
   c. hungrily   h. thickly
   d. lazily   i. slowly
   e. loosely   j. easily
4. Answers will vary.
5. a. opened   d. looked
   b. play   e. is raining
   c. turned
6. a. gently   d. Carefully
   b. proud   e. strong
   c. cheaply
7. a. We went outside to play in our tree house.
   b. Bees buzzed noisily around the hive.
   c. The cup fell down and broke.
   d. The bird flew away into a tall tree.
   e. The sun shone brightly in the blue sky.

SENTENCES

Student Page 47 (page 89)

1. a. Sunflowers grow in the field.
   d. Pass the salt.
   e. Let's go fly our kites.
   g. Start the motor, please.
   i. I can't play hopscotch.
   j. Go away.
2. Rhys and Ella are brother and sister. Rhys is eight and Ella is ten. They live on a farm. Before school, they feed the hens. After school, they bring the cows home for milking.
3. Answers will vary.

Student Page 48 (page 90)

1. Answers will vary.
2. a. fact   d. opinion
   b. opinion   e. opinion
   c. fact
3. Answers will vary.

Student Page 49 (page 91)

1. a. A table has four legs.
   b. You would find pages and writing in a book.

c. You buy a parrot from a pet store.
   d. A ruler is 12 inches long.
2. Answers will vary.

Student Page 50 (page 92)

1. a. We have dinner at seven o'clock.
   b. Everybody stand back!
   c. What a wonderful surprise!
   d. Let's go swimming in the pool.
   e. Look behind you!
2. Answers will vary.
3. Drawings will vary.

Student Page 51 (page 93)

1. a. Throw   d. Hang
   b. Make   e. Turn
   c. Carry
Every sentence begins with the verb.
2. Answers will vary.
3. Answers will vary.

Student Page 52 (page 94)

1. a. A honeybee flew
   b. The little kitten sleeps
   c. The school bus stopped
   d. My uncle lives
   e. The fat, brown spider spun
2. Answers will vary.

Student Page 53 (page 95)

1. a. The wheat in the field is ripe and golden.
   b. Wind filled the sails of the ship.
   c. The freight train sped along the railway lines.
   d. Dad and Uncle Bill cooked meat on the barbeque.
   e. You may see a rainbow after the rain.
   f. Soft, white snowflakes fell silently all night.
2. a. The rancher   d. The children
   b. our team   e. the spider
   c. Sunflowers   f. Your backpack

Student Page 54 (page 96)

1. Answers will vary.
2. Answers will vary.

Student Page 55 (page 97)

1. a. and   d. but
   b. but   e. so
   c. so   f. and
2. a. Tom wants to go in the pool, but he can't swim.
   b. Mia has black hair, and Jacqui is blonde.
   c. The bell has rung, so you may go home.
   d. Greg knocked on the door, but no one answered.
   e. I like coffee, and I also like tea.
   f. It rained heavily, so the water tank is full.

Student Page 56 (page 98)

1. a. "I can't find my other sock"—Katy
   b. "Did you look under your bed?"—Mom

c. "Have you looked in the sock drawer?"—Sue
   d. "It's probably in the hamper."—Dad
   e. "Oh, here it is. It was in my other shoe."—Katy
2. a. "Would you like me to read another story?"
   b. "Thank you for being so kind."
   c. "Get out of my way!"
   d. "Do you have a new bike, William?"
   e. "It's raining," "Let's go inside."

Assessment—Sentences (pages 99–101)

1. a. Wheat is growing in the field.
   d. Wait for me.
   e. Let's have some ice cream.
   g. Cut two pieces of string.
   i. She doesn't like olives.
2. a. The men   d. The crowd
   b. the soup   e. Only five people
   c. Jasmine
3. a. What did you eat for lunch today?
   b. How do you make paper planes?
   c. Why are you wearing a backpack?
4. Answers will vary.
5. a. Wash   b. Cut   c. Feed
6. a. Slice some cheese for our sandwiches.
   b. Put on your socks and shoes.
7. a. and   b. but   c. so
8. a. Joy bought a brush, and she also bought a comb.
   b. I wanted to read my book, but I left it at home.
9. "Where will I pin up my picture?" Bobby asked the teacher.
   The teacher replied, "Please put it on the wall near the door."
10. Answers will vary.
11. Answers will vary.
12. An emu is an Australia bird. It has wings, but it cannot fly. Have you ever seen one?

WORDWORKS TASK CARDS (pages 105–109)

1. cooking pot, swimming pool, running shoes, caring person, crowded street, loaded truck, baked beans, roasted peanuts
2. lost/found, fresh/stale, smooth/rough, late/early, sharp/dull, old/young, high/low, east/west
3. seen, see, saw, seen, seen, see, saw
4. coastline, homework, headlights, firewood, driveway, popcorn, bedroom, cornflakes
5. slithering snake, crunchy apple, funny clown, sharp pencil, dangerous fire, heavy log, elderly person, sour lemon
6. Nouns—kitchen, boat, football, clock, candle, computer, people, kangaroo
   Adjectives—happy, busy, crunchy, long, large, lazy, sweet, simple
7. Nouns—riddle, kettle, title, jungle, table
   Verbs—stumble, sizzle, juggle, struggle, dazzle

8. they're = they are, we've = we have, I've = I have, they'd = they would, it's = it is, can't = cannot, won't = will not, couldn't = could not, don't = do not, hasn't = has not

9. Answers will vary.

10. happily, easily, gladly, gently, quickly, noisily, hungrily, safely, lazily, usually, mostly, brightly

11. did, were, had, found, grew, cried, hopped, rung, was, fell, sat, saw

12. running, liking, drying, snowing, sitting, leaving, tumbling, crashing, bending, cutting, deciding, washing

13. Nouns—pie, tale, garden, angel, spaceship, pickle, prince, violin

    Adjectives—warm, enormous, sunny, interesting, helpful, careless, friendly, tasty

14. Answers will vary.

15. Answers will vary.

16. did, done, done, did, done, did

17. postcard, toothpick, goalkeeper, handbag, broomstick, football, raindrops, eyelashes

18. grapes, pencils, babies, children, bananas, leaves, women, passengers

19. Answers will vary.

20. Ducks and geese, hat, tigers, Writing, road, Bob and I, Mary, Everyone

21. Male—nephew, rooster, husband, uncle Female—cow, niece, queen, aunt Either—teacher, athlete, adult, pilot

22. you've = you have, I'll = I will, she's = she is, they're = they are, we're = we are, you're = you are, I'm = I am, he'd = he had, didn't = did not, hadn't = had not, wouldn't = would not, doesn't = does not, aren't = are not, weren't = were not, can't = cannot, wasn't = was not

23. Saying—stammer, say, chat, grumble, boast Doing—sprint, travel, boil, sail, build

24. Answers will vary.

25. Animal—monkey, koala, zebra, deer Person—dentist, gymnast, pilot, gardener Place—supermarket, park, India, kitchen Thing—spade, fence, ladder, torch

26. tame/wild, honest/dishonest, fast/slow, straight/crooked, long/short, wide/narrow

27. gone, went, went, gone, gone, went, Gone

28. am, has, will, is, can, are

29. Person—clever, strong, friendly, helpful Place—crowded, grassy, sandy, rocky Thing—plastic, striped, broken, tasty

30. She will = She'll, I have = I've, He is = He's, You are = You're, We have = We've, I would = I'd, They are = They're, She would = She'd, I am = I'm, It is = It's, You have = You've, We are = We're

GRAMMAR BY NUMBERS CARDS (pages 134–143)

Grammar By Numbers 1 (Nouns)
1. newspaper
2. cows
3. jam
4. plants
5. key
6. oranges
7. door
8. finger
9. candle
10. umbrella

Grammar By Numbers 2 (Adjectives)
1. blue
2. wooden
3. thick
4. juicy
5. disappointed
6. leafy
7. slippery
8. racing
9. little
10. dirty

Grammar By Numbers 3 (Pronouns)
1. his
2. mine
3. their
4. you
5. it
6. my
7. our
8. us

Grammar By Numbers 4 (Verbs)
1. cracked
2. gobbled
3. throw
4. will chop
5. is writing
6. Wash
7. have done
8. smashed
9. is filling
10. were
11. shouted

Grammar By Numbers 5 (Adverbs)
1. quickly
2. slowly
3. outside
4. later
5. east
6. When
7. tightly
8. sideways
9. loudly
10. quietly
11. Sometimes

Grammar By Numbers 6 (Contractions)
1. don't
2. can't
3. Let's
4. What's
5. it's
6. wasn't
7. didn't
8. There's
9. haven't
10. They've
11. She's
12. Who's

Grammar By Numbers 7 (Antonyms)
1. down
2. slow
3. happy
4. wide
5. old
6. tall
7. short
8. dirty
9. fresh
10. rough
11. young
12. over
13. leaves

Grammar By Numbers 8 (Compound Nouns)
1. cowboy
2. headlights
3. windmill
4. scarecrow
5. goalkeeper
6. bathroom
7. cardboard
8. sunset
9. baseball
10. footpath
11. runway
12. handbag

Grammar By Numbers 9 (Question Words)
1. What
2. Why
3. How
4. Where
5. Who
6. Which
7. Whose
8. When

Grammar By Numbers 10 (Verbs)
1. Wash
2. Sing
3. Count
4. Look
5. Paint
6. Switch
7. Add
8. Read
9. Turn
10. Plant
11. Take
12. Write
13. Wait
14. Close

KRISS KROSS PUZZLES (pages 144–149)

Kriss Kross 1

```
P R Y U S F G B E D
U F K L K B T X E L
M G R W A E E M V G
P T E J S K R Y D A
K Q T H E R S G D T
I C U P B O A R D E
N S P H O H B R Z D
D F M J A L K R S T
N H O U R E F T Y X
D F C H D R E A M Y
```

Kriss Kross 2

```
P R T U S F G P R D
E F R L K E F I N K
F G A W A E C H V G
F T M J T S E S M L
A Q P A L M G H A K
R C O P B O A R M E
I F L O W E R Z M D
G C I B A N A N A Y
N H N U R E G T L X
D N E I R F P T M Y
```

Kriss Kross 3

```
N I F F U M N B E M
U F K L K B E T Z A
M R O T C O D U R C
P T E J T S R K Y H
W Q C H E R A K D I
O B A N D A G E N N
D S R H O C B Y Z E
A F P R I N C E S S
H G E U R E F T Y X
S F T R U M P E T Y
```

Kriss Kross 4

```
P R T U S E N A L P
U F E L K B T X E L
M G A L F E R M V G
P T C A R R O T Y A
K Q H O U S E G X B
K C C E P B H A R D R E
C A S R H O E R Z E A
R F M J A D K R S A
T I B B A R F T C D
D F N U D H S U R B
```

ANSWER KEY

Kriss Kross 5

```
S P H I K O H I G H
U O D D K B T S F L
M W R I Y E B F R A
P E A J L S N R I B
K R T H E R S G E L
I F E W V O A R N U
N U G N I C N A D T
D L M J L T K R L Y
N H N E Z O R F Y X
R O U N D G I J L Y
```

Kriss Kross 9

```
E R K B E L I E V E
S H O V E O T X R U
M O R H A S E M V S
P G E H T E K R Y U
K R T H I V S B D B
S O M E R S A U L T
N W O R R O B Y Z R
D F M J A L A R S A
N H O U R E K T R C
D F W R I T E L M T
```

Kriss Kross 13

```
A R Y U S F W K E D
T O L D K B S A I D
E G R W A S E M V E
P M E N D E D R Y B
K I T L E H S T D B
I C F P B U A N D B
N S P A I N T E D R
D F M J A G O W R E
E D O R R E F L E R
D F C H D R O I W R
```

Kriss Kross 6

```
H R Y M F U N N Y D
C I F K A K B I X O
I G R E N A E U C N
R T E T N Y W I D E
K Q T H E R S S D T
S T R O N G K U N G
N S P H O H C N O D
O D A Z Z L I N G N
N H O U R E U Y I N
D F C J D R Q I S Y
```

Kriss Kross 10

```
O R E U C S E R P D
R F K L K B T I D O
E M W R I P E A S I
M O A G R E E K R S
O I T H E V A E L T
V U P L R T R I W A
E S P H S P E A K L
U F M J A L K R E L
N H O U R E F T Y K
D S C R E A M A I X
```

Kriss Kross 14

```
P E N B L E W H E D
R F G R K B T Z J L
M S H O W E D M V D
P T E U T N K R Y E
K I S T G E D S G D
I W U H B E A M A N
F E L T O D B A Z L
D P M J A L K D S P
N T O K I C K E D
O D E S S A P A I V
```

Kriss Kross 7

```
E R Y L U F E S U F
L F K L S L X E A B
D G R W A S I M V U
E R T J V E B H H L
R Q E T I L O P A O
L C L A B P M R D U
Y A L L H E A V Y S
D F A L H F T Y X
N H C U R H F T Y X
L O S A L T Y L E S
```

Kriss Kross 11

```
S R Y U S F G P U T
T F K L K B T X E L
A G O R I D E M V G
Y T E J T S E R Y L
K F T H W A S H D I
I O G P A O A Y D F
N S P H N H B R Z F
D F M J T L K R S T
N H O U R D E E N
A R E H D R Z A T I
```

Kriss Kross 15

```
P R E U S C G A E D
T F W L D I E D B L
M G A I R J E D V G
P T S T O P P E D A
D E B T H V R S D W
E C U P E O A R D E
K S P G I H B U Z R
R X F E L L K R G
A H I U T E F T V X
M D E N A O R G I S
```

Kriss Kross 8

```
L R H U S F C B Y D
C F S E N A U G H T Y
C G T R J I S O R I
A R E J W A E S O W M
R E J F A M O U S M A
E L T I P B I R X E
L E S R H E H B R E
S F M J D L K R D
S H I U U E F T Y X
D B E A R D E D M B
```

Kriss Kross 12

```
D E E L B I O R T D
I O G S D T H N O E
E S M I F E E L V C
P T I J T S K R Y I
K E X P L A I N T D
I A U P B M A R D E
L L P S O H B R Z I
L E F G N I R B R S T
A H O X R E F T Y X
K F C H D R T A L K
```

Kriss Kross 16

```
S H O O K F G B W I
U F K L K B T U R L
J U M P E D E M O G
P D E A T B E N T A
K E K D D E O S G E
I O U P D L O G B R
N O M L E S H O N E
N C O D E T L E M
D F C H C I E X S Z
```

Kriss Kross 17

```
U R Y A W A G B T Y
P S L I K B O X O L
M D L T A E U I M O
B R U J T S T R O P
I A F N O O S G R E
K W E P B O I U R E
Z K P H Y L D U O L
D C O J A L E R W S
N A H E R E H W O N
D B S Y A W E D I S
```

Kriss Kross 18

```
S R E A R L Y B I R
U F K N K B M X G L
I T R Y A E O S E U
F O R W A R D S N T
K D T H E R L G T L
I A U E B W E L L I
D Y P R O H S R Y S
O F M E J L K R S I
W H O U R E E C N O
N F C H D I J A X N
```

Kriss Kross 19

```
X S O M E T I M E S
U D F L V B N I T L
R G T U E Z S P A G
P T E J R Y E P L I
K A N H Y R D E E B
E L S E W H E R E K
N W P I H E B R I C
D A T H E R E I S I
N Y O U R E F L Y M
D S C F E R D Y M Q
```

Kriss Kross 20

```
F A S T S F H G I H
M Y L E N O L X S Y
U L R W G E A M V A
P N E V E R T R Y D
T E T H I X E G A R
O D U P H E R E F T
N D P H O H B R T S
Q U I E T L Y R E E
N S O M E W H E R E
D F C H K R J A M Y
```

Kriss Kross 21

```
G E Y A I U O Y T Y
E W L I K B U X O L
M D T S A E R I M I
X T H E M I T R O R
U A E N I L S R G R
L D Y Z N U I E R S
N K P H E E W H O L
S C O J A L K D H T
H A B D F Y E H T N
E B S Y A F E D I S
```

Kriss Kross 22

```
I R E S R F Y B T R
U F K N K B M X H L
I T R H I M O S E U
M O R E A R D S I Y
E D T R E R L G R L
I A U S B F E H S I
D I P R O H S C Y S
O T M E J L K I S I
W S O U R S E H E O
N F C S D I J W X N
```

Kriss Kross 23

```
S U O M E G X H E B
H D W H A T N I T U
E G T U E H E P S S
P Y E J R E I M L Y
I O N H Y I D E R L
T X S E W R E W I K
S F P I H E M E H T
H A T S E R E I S Y
I Y O T R E F O Y O
S P C I E R D W I U
```

Kriss Kross 24

```
F I T S S F W G I H
U Y L E N O H I S I
S L R W G E O M H M
H N Y O U R S R M Y
E D T H I X E G A R
I D U P H E R E T T
N D M I N E B R T T
T J Y E T L E R E S
T S O M E W H P I H
D F C O U R S A M Y
```

GRAMMAR TASK CARDS (pages 150–161)

Nouns 1

1. Places—school, desert, garden, street, beach; Things—blanket, fence, door, soap, candle
2. Nouns will vary.

Nouns 2

1. a. pigs   f. boats
   b. roses   g. foxes
   c. babies   h. calves
   d. lemons   i. teeth
   e. benches

2. a. Mr. Baxter lives in Sandgate.
   b. Jim's birthday is in July, and Sam's is in April.
   c. Our boat sailed down the Colorado River and under London Bridge.
   d. Our friends from Arizona visit us at Christmas time.
   e. The Olympic Games were held in Beijing.

Nouns 3

1. Suggested answers: doorway, network, footpath, footwork, landslide, waterslide, pathway, homework, homeland, runway, landmark, bookwork, bookmark, waterway, watermark

2. a. an elephant's trunk
   b. the old man's beard
   c. some birds' beaks
   d. someone's hat
   e. a dog's paws
   f. our friends' bikes
   g. children's books
   h. a lizard's skin
   i. hens' eggs
   j. a pin's head

Nouns 4

1. a. an, the   d. an, an
   b. The, a   e. An, the
   c. a, the

2. a. queen   f. woman
   b. mare   g. cow
   c. goose   h. hen
   d. lady   i. sister
   e. aunt   j. princess

Adjectives 1

1. Answers will vary.
2. Answers will vary.

Adjectives 2

1. People—serious, clever, rich, helpful, worried, friendly, lonely, brave; Things—plastic, wobbly, wide, crushed, tin, useful, green, straw

2. crackling fire, gardening gloves, swimming pool, potted plant, melted ice, branded cows

3. large, salty, important, exciting, crunchy, unusual—Sentences will vary.

ANSWER KEY

Adjectives 3

1. cloudy, hot, cooler, new, red, soft, cool, warm, refreshing, good
2. a. fat, fatter, fattest
   b. happy, happier, happiest
   c. safe, safer, safest
   d. old, older, oldest

Adjectives 4

1. happy/sad, young/old, stale/fresh, slow/fast or quick, long/short, narrow/wide, bright/dull, sour/sweet, heavy/light, safe/dangerous, clean/dirty, weak/strong, small/large or big, low/high
2. a. high, higher, highest
   b. angry, angrier, angriest
   c. clean, cleaner, cleanest
   d. grand, grander, grandest

Pronouns 1

1. a. I   d. I
   b. me   e. me
   c. I, me
2. a. There   d. there
   b. their   e. There, their
   c. their

Pronouns 2

1. a. She waited for her friend by the school gate.
   b. Dad went fishing with his friends.
   c. The twins bought a bunch of flowers for their mother.
   d. I like pizza. (also We, They)
   e. We called out to them as they came around the bend.
2. a. Who   d. Who
   b. Which   e. Whose
   c. What

Pronouns 3

1. a. your/our/their
   b. mine (hers, his, yours)
   c. his
   d. our
   e. mine (his, hers, ours, theirs)
   f. my
   g. our
2. a. They   d. you
   b. its   e. He
   c. She

Pronouns 4

1. Answers will vary.
2. a. Josh   d. The children
   b. teacher   e. Marty
   c. Priya   f. team

Verbs 1

1. a. did   e. did
   b. done   f. done
   c. done   g. done
   d. Did   h. done
2. a. went   e. went
   b. gone   f. gone
   c. gone   g. went
   d. went   h. gone

Verbs 2

1. a. saw   e. saw
   b. seen   f. saw
   c. saw   g. seen
   d. seen   h. saw
2. speak, stir, sneeze, bite, drive, drip, have, seize, sleep, build

Verbs 3

1. a. bought   f. sat
   b. wore   g. patted
   c. saw   h. dried
   d. bent   i. walked
   e. stood   j. waved
2. a. didn't   g. won't
   b. couldn't   h. wasn't
   c. hasn't   i. aren't
   d. can't   j. haven't
   e. isn't   k. don't
   f. wouldn't   l. weren't

Verbs 4

1. walking, looking, carrying, trotting, rolled, barked, running, splashing, picked, washed
2. a. she'll   g. they're
   b. they've   h. he'd
   c. you're   i. she's
   d. he's   j. we'd
   e. we're   k. I'm
   f. I'd   l. we'll

Adverbs 1

1. Answers will vary.
2. a. strongly   d. later
   b. backwards   e. faster, faster
   c. up, up, up

Adverbs 2

1. a. largely   f. lazily
   b. steadily   g. famously
   c. grandly   h. joyfully
   d. lately   i. softly
   e. narrowly   j. happily
2. a. Where   d. Why
   b. How   e. Where
   c. When

Adverbs 3

1. a. heavily   d. roughly
   b. wearily   e. badly
   c. quick
2. Sentences will vary.

Adverbs 4

1. a. when   d. when
   b. how   e. how
   c. where
2. a. crept   d. leave
   b. fell   e. buy
   c. chattered

Sentences 1

1. Sammy went to visit his Aunt Nell at her little beach house. He had a room upstairs overlooking the water. Sammy and his aunt swam every day. They gathered seaweed and shells. Aunt Nell's dog was always nearby.

2. a. played   d. sits
   b. glittered   e. are skiing
   c. fell

Sentences 2

Answers will vary.

Sentences 3

1. a. I like apples, but Paul likes plums.
   b. It is late, so I must leave.
   c. I ate a cupcake, and I drank a glass of milk.
   d. We would like to stay, but we have to catch a train.
   e. He stood up, so he could be seen.
2. a. The boy at the desk was writing a story.
   b. My yellow kite hit the top of a tree.
   c. Every morning, I eat eggs for breakfast.
   d. The black spider spun a large web.
   e. In the race, Jessie fell and cut her knee.

Sentences 4

1. a. We went to the airport to watch the planes.
   b. Have you been to the zoo to see the crocodiles?
   c. You're in trouble!
   d. Collect the eggs from the henhouse, please.
   e. Will you play chess with me?
2. a.   "Happy birthday, Liz," said her mom, handing her a little box.
        "Oh, thank you, Mom," she replied, opening her gift. "This is beautiful!" she said, holding up the gold necklace.
        "Have you seen my kitten, Mrs. Johns?" asked Toby.
        Mrs. Johns replied, "Yes, I just saw her jump the back fence."